A GLITCH IN THE MATRIX

A GLITCH IN THE MATRIX

TALES OF THE UNEXPLAINABLE UNREAL

JESSICA CASTRO
AKA AUNTIE MATRIX

STERLING ETHOS
New York

STERLING ETHOS
New York

ISBN 978-1-4549-5606-8
ISBN 978-1-4549-5607-5 (e-book)

Library of Congress Control Number: 2024932186

For information about custom editions, special sales, and premium
purchases, please contact specialsales@unionsquareandco.com.

Printed in Canada

2 4 6 8 10 9 7 5 3 1

unionsquareandco.com

Cover design by Jack Smyth
Cover photo courtesy of the Author
Interior design by Kevin Ullrich

To anyone who has experienced something they cannot explain: we believe you.

CONTENTS

INTRODUCTION
A Glitch in the Matrix

"From there to here, from here to there, funny things are everywhere." Our beloved rhyming children's author Dr. Seuss had it *almost* right. I would personally replace the word "funny" with the phrase "jaw-dropping, unexplainable, and sometimes creepy." At least that's what all the stories I have received suggest.

You see, although I haven't had many noteworthy experiences myself, I kind of . . . collect them. Maybe the fact that I haven't seen an actual ghost or heard an actual skinwalker or had an actual premonition is the very reason I am so intrigued by these stories. At the end of the day, I'm just a gal with a social media account who is obsessed with all things supernatural, and who now has thousands of emails from fans detailing their most odd true tales; some of the best of which make up this book.

I started a TikTok account for fun in August 2021. I nervously posted a duet, followed by a video of me speaking about the loneliness of spiritual awakening. To my bewilderment, I got an overwhelming response from people mirroring my exact feelings. The video went viral (80k views, which is certainly not in the millions, but was INSANE to me at the time), and I felt seen and understood for probably the first time in my life. Who knew that an app I thought was for dancing children could offer such a community of like-minded individuals, and provide a place to be myself, to learn and to grow?

One day in November 2022 I was reading "glitch in the matrix" stories online, and, thinking they were fascinating and that my followers might enjoy them, I posted a video of myself reading a few. They loved it. So I posted another. They still loved it. By the second or third video in the series, people had started asking where they could send me *their* stories.

And so I started reading stories submitted by fans. In Part 21 of my video series, I used a reply comment from someone calling me "Auntie Matrix." I mentioned that I loved the nickname. Everyone started using it, and it stuck.

If you are unaware, a "glitch in the matrix" is an experience that seems strange or unusual. A moment that feels like it is not quite real, or that it is a glitch in the reality that we perceive. The term is often used to describe things like time losses or jumps, moments of déjà vu, disappearing or reappearing items, etc.

The stories I was receiving quickly began to branch out from true glitches in the matrix to other related areas such as aliens, dreams, premonitions, and the paranormal. After executing a poll among fans, the phrase "Let's Read Some Glitch in the Matrix Stories" was kept as my intro, even though the stories now encompassed many other things.

I quickly learned that this niche has an incredibly large audience of believers who are extremely passionate about these subjects. I also started getting very heartfelt comments and emails about how

I have touched or helped people in different ways. Apparently my voice is extremely soothing and, despite the creepy nature of the stories, helps people and their children to fall asleep. They enjoy and appreciate my authenticity, and I am constantly told that I make people feel heard and validated in their experiences. I have had countless people say they have never shared their stories with anyone for fear of judgment and rejection. It is known and articulated frequently that in our little community that we have built, we believe you.

Reading these stories has not only made so many feel validated, but has also opened many eyes and minds in the collective, helping people to awaken and realize that we are not just this one human existence. There have been numerous times where a story I have read has sparked a memory in someone else, who is now eager to share *their* experience. I strongly feel I am helping people to awaken, learn, grow, heal, feel accepted and seen, and become confident in themselves and the truth of their experiences—which is part of what I feel I am put on this earth to do. I fiercely believe that I am not only entertaining people, but helping many in this capacity.

Maybe you yourself have had an unexplainable experience. Or maybe you picked up this book simply because you love anything that creeps you out. Either way, buckle up, because shit's about to get weird.

This book is a compilation of some of the best stories I have read since I started this whole thing. I think the scariest part is that these are *true* stories from *real* people. These are not movies, shows, or works of fiction thought up by some super-creative and imaginative minds. They actually happened. I don't know about you, but for me that really ups the creep factor.

If you are going on this journey with me, I think it's important to understand a few things. If you are already very well versed in weirdness, please feel free to skip ahead and enjoy the stories. Otherwise, I am going to go into a little bit of detail about some stuff that you might read.

What is a "glitch in the matrix"?

There are a lot of people out there who believe in simulation theory. Simulation theory is the idea that what people perceive as reality is actually an advanced, hyper-realistic computer simulation (the matrix), potentially overseen by a higher being. That we are basically all just characters in a video game. Think of a glitch in the matrix as a glitch in a video game—when something weird happens that doesn't make sense according to the laws of physics. In a video game, you might see a character "glitching out" walk through a wall, skip from one location to another in an instant, stuck in some kind of loop, etc. Real-life glitches in the matrix are the same thing. People have experienced items disappearing and then reappearing in different locations—like the woman who dropped her phone lying in bed and found it on the front seat of her car. Some have experienced items multiplying—like the lady who found a second set of the same thrift-store baby shoes in a different room of her house—same markings on both pairs. Or the one that all of a sudden had two of the same exact vacuum cleaners, when she previously had only one. Many have experienced time losses or time jumps (both forward and backward) that they cannot explain. I was sent one video where a woman was frozen in place in a very unnatural position, and another where someone seemed to be stuck in an infinite loop getting in and out of a car the same exact way every time. And then there are the multiple videos of planes literally frozen in the air, which is something I have actually seen myself.

Another very common occurrence that is considered a glitch in the matrix is déjà vu. If you remember the original movie *The Matrix*, Neo sees a black cat and then sees the same black cat again. He is told that having déjà vu means they have "changed something" in the matrix (in this case, it was to slow their escape). While we humans in "real" life experiencing déjà vu may not mean the same thing, you have to admit that it does feel like you may have skipped back in time just a few seconds and are going through that moment again.

The "matrix" itself is interpreted differently by different people. There are those who believe it is governed by some higher power. There are those who claim it is just like the movie, in which we have been enslaved by machines. And there are those who think that every person is living in their own "matrix," which they are creating and projecting with their own thoughts.

And what matrix would be complete without NPCs? An NPC is a term used in the video-game world, and it stands for non-player character or non-playable character. In other words, it's any character in a game that is not controlled by a player. It is referring to those characters in a video game that can be found in the same exact spot all the time, doing the same preprogrammed set of actions and saying the same collection of phrases. An example of this in real life would be the person who swears that their neighborhood is their own little simulation. They see things like the same person in the same outfit walking the same dog every time they leave their house, no matter the hour.

Some are very strict with the term "glitch in the matrix," but I feel that it encompasses a lot more than just the traditional definition. When it comes down to it, not one of us actually knows the truth. What many believe are ghosts or spirits may actually just be people in another timeline or dimension who are bleeding over into ours for the moment—either on purpose or by some weird accidental glitch in the fabric of the universe. Speaking of timelines. . . .

What is quantum immortality?

Multiverse theory is the idea that there is not just one universe, but a near-infinite number of universes. Together, these universes are presumed to make up everything that exists. Since there are so many, the thought exists that many of these universes (or timelines) can be nearly identical to each other. And so if we were to find ourselves moved to one of the closest timelines, we might not even notice. Some people believe that we are constantly switching timelines with the choices we make, and that it is even possible to do so consciously.

There is a big conspiracy theory that we as a planet switched into another universe in 2012 when CERN turned on the Large Hadron Collider (LHC). CERN is the European Organization for Nuclear Research, and they operate the largest particle-physics laboratory in the world. The LHC is the world's largest and highest-energy particle collider. It accelerates particles such as protons close to the speed of light, and they collide with other protons. When CERN turned on the LHC in 2012, they discovered the long-sought-after Higgs boson, but many people believe they also destroyed our universe and threw us into a different timeline. This event is thought to be the reason behind all the Mandela effects that we now experience.

If you are not aware, a Mandela effect is a situation in which a large mass of people believes that something is one way, when it is in fact another. The name stems from the fact that many people (including myself) swear that Nelson Mandela died in prison in the 1980s. He apparently actually died in 2013. Examples of the Mandela effect include the very popular children's book series *The Berenstein Bears* actually being spelled Berenstain (with an "a" instead of an "e"), Curious George apparently *not* having a tail, and the Monopoly Man never sporting a monocle.

If an entire planet can "die" and switch timelines, why can't it happen to just one single person? This is the theory of quantum immortality. Quantum immortality is the thought that when we die, we actually just jump to the nearest possible timeline. Most times, we do not even remember it happening, as it seems to be accompanied by some sort of backward time jump or memory loss. For example, when you *almost* got in that fatal car accident? Maybe you actually *did*, but instead of going to heaven or hell or some astral plane, you just jumped to the nearest timeline, and it was *so* similar to your previous one that you don't even notice. But there are some people, like you will read about in the pages ahead, who experience that accident, the whole bloody thing, and are then teleported back in time to right before it happens. Were they shown this by some higher being of light so they make a different choice and the accident never takes place at all? Or have they actually died and been thrown into an alternate universe, and in that timeline the accident was just a "close call"? Some might argue that the people in these stories are not actually experiencing the traumatizing event, but having a premonition.

What is a premonition?

A premonition can be as simple as having a very strong gut feeling that something bad is going to happen, or it can be as detailed as having such an intense vision of the actual event that you are not sure whether you really experienced it or not. So maybe the person who saw and felt themselves die in that car accident actually only saw it in their head, and it wasn't taking place in this physical reality. Maybe they were shown this scenario so they could avoid it and get out of harm's way. Many people have premonitions in their dreams—they will dream of something and it will end up happening shortly afterward, in waking life. If this happens often, it can be very stressful, especially if the premonitions are negative in nature, and especially if they are about other people. Some, however, have these visions while they are awake, perhaps like the person who remembers experiencing that car accident even though it "never happened." Speaking of things that never happened. . . .

Can aliens erase our memory?

An extremely common theme in most alien-abduction stories is time loss or loss of memory. Many of those who recall seeing an actual extraterrestrial being or an Unidentified Anomalous Phenomenon (UAP, formerly known as UFO or Unidentified Flying Object), report a significant loss of time. One may be driving down the road, look up to see a UAP, then look back down at the dashboard to notice that a few *hours* have passed. It is believed that the beings are erasing your memory, because the experience of being abducted can be exceptionally stressful and traumatizing mentally, emotionally, and sometimes even physically. Signs of abduction can include time loss, memory loss, or even randomly finding markings on the body possibly indicative of some sort of injection. So, was that "glitch in the matrix" where you lost five hours a true glitch, or were you abducted?

What other beings are there besides aliens?

So many. There are way too many to list here in entirety, but I will give you quick names and definitions of a handful.

Skinwalker

A skinwalker can be found in Native American folklore and is believed to be a powerful witch who has the ability to turn into, possess, or disguise themselves as any animal they desire. They are often described as having glowing eyes and a twisted, hunched-over appearance. They are incredibly fast and strong and are most active at night, often targeting travelers, campers, and the like.

Wendigo

A wendigo is a cannibalistic shapeshifter from Algonquian folklore primarily found in the northern forests of the United States and Canada. It is a tall, thin, emaciated humanoid creature with a deer skull for a head, razor-sharp teeth, and glowing eyes. Both skin-walkers and wendigos are known to often use the sounds of their last victims to lure more unexpecting victims to kill. So if you're outside alone at night and you hear someone scream for help, no, you didn't.

Hat Man

The Hat Man is one of the most commonly seen sleep-paralysis demons in the world. He is an unnaturally tall, thin, shadow figure of a man wearing a hat. He has no discernible facial features, but is often reported having red, glowing eyes. He is mainly seen right before you fall asleep or right after you wake up. Sometimes he is standing in the corner of the room or at the foot of the bed, and many times is observed during sleep paralysis. There have been reports that if you see him during the day, it normally means that you or someone around you is about to die.

Doppelgänger

A doppelgänger is an entity that will take on the appearance of someone that you know, live with, or care about in order to lure you in to them. For example, your partner comes home from work, walks past you, and goes to take a shower. You then get a call from your *actual* partner, letting you know that they are on their way; and when you go check the bathroom, the other "them" is nowhere to be found.

Mimic

A mimic is kind of like a doppelgänger, but instead of trying to lure you in by taking on someone's appearance, they will take on someone's voice. You may hear your mom calling you from the basement, when she is actually in the next room.

This is only the tip of the iceberg when it comes to supernatural beings. I will allow you to go down that rabbit hole for yourself. For now, the information I have touched upon here should allow you to go into reading these stories with a little bit of knowledge to help you draw your own conclusions. So sit back, grab a snack, and let's get weird.

WEIRD THINGS BEGAN TO HAPPEN TO ME . . .

Where's Allan?

SUBMITTED BY UNCLE NEZER

Second things first. I didn't enjoy writing this down in detail. I didn't like writing this down at all. I don't like this story. I don't like thinking about it. I don't like talking about it. I've sent some other stories, and, to put it into perspective, those stories were scary, spooky, or a little supernatural, but I got through them and moved on without any issues. This is the *only* experience I've *ever* had that has given me nightmares. I talked about it with my wife last night, deciding whether to write and submit it. Even though we only talked about it and this happened decades ago, I barely slept last night. After writing it today, I likely won't sleep well for the next few nights.

Now, first things second: the story. I grew up as a logger and as such I've spent a *lot* of time in the woods. I've been through and seen some super-weird and scary stuff. When I was twenty-two, I was still working for my father's logging company. My cousin David and I worked as a two-man team. We didn't live on the mountain as I'd done some summers, but we spent most of that logging season in the woods. David was an avid hunter and, as the season wound down, he wanted to spend most of the evenings after work scouting for game. A lot of loggers did this, and some of them even turned their knowledge of game whereabouts into profit as hunting guides.

This particular timber sale (the area where we harvested the trees) was on what we called the back side, meaning the north side of the mountain range, way back by a government-designated wilderness area. One Friday after work, David again wanted to scout for game, so we loaded into his green beat-up country-boy truck and off we went. Over the summer there had been a couple of reports of a troublesome animal in the area, so, when we left the truck, we both took small .22 caliber rifles just in case.

We scouted the area he wanted and headed back to his truck as the evening started to turn dark. To make the return trip faster and easier, we were walking through a large patch about four hundred yards long where a forest fire had gone through a few years previous, called a "burn." We knew the truck was parked on the road only fifty yards or so through the trees that had been untouched at the other end of the burn.

David was the first to hear something over to our right. If a tree falls in the forest but you don't see it, it still makes a sound. We looked over but didn't see anything, so we kept walking. We both heard the next crash. A scorched tree on the edge of the burn had fallen into the open area. We didn't think much of it and laughed at ourselves for being so jumpy. That's when we noticed the shape in the trees. It was just far enough back in the tree line to obscure any details. It was getting dark, the shape was moving the same direction as we were, it was *very* tall, and it was walking upright. A bear can walk on its hind legs for short distances, but whatever this was kept pace with us for around three hundred yards. If we slowed down or sped up, so did it. We kept our rifles at the ready and continued toward the truck. Then we noticed a problem.

Essentially, the burn was shaped like a tear or water drop, and we were walking toward the narrow end. As the burn narrowed, we were on a collision course with whatever was shadowing our movements—and it was getting darker. Whatever it was never attacked us, and we never saw more than a large dark shape, but we could hear it crashing through the trees and underbrush right up until we literally jumped into David's truck and flew out of there. When I told my dad about it later, he just nodded and said quite a few stories like that had come out of that general area.

Monday rolled around as it always does, and we headed back up the mountain. When we stopped for lunch, we were greeted at our landing (logging base of operations) by a forest ranger. David and I knew him as Mr. Johnson from seventh-grade history. He said Allan, a logger from a timber sale a couple miles off, had gone missing over the weekend. Allan was well known and fairly well liked, but he did have a reputation for drinking. The prevailing theory was that he'd gotten drunk and wandered too far from camp. The sheriff's department had asked the Forest Service to help look for him, and the Forest Service was asking all the other loggers in the general vicinity if we'd seen Allan and basically pressed us all into service as an unofficial search-and-rescue effort.

Ranger Johnson gave us a government-issue hand-held GPS and asked us to search the area between our logging site and the one Allan's company was working. GPS was relatively new at that time, so the ranger gave us a thirty-second how-to on it. If we found Allan and he was injured or couldn't get out for some reason, we were supposed to mark the spot with the GPS, then come back out and find a ranger. Rangers all had CB radios in their trucks and could call the sheriff's department for assistance. We got the instruction that in the worst case, if he was dead, *do not* touch him, mark the spot, and get the rangers and sheriff.

David and I headed out, just far enough apart to still be able to see each other while also covering more ground than we would if we walked together. As the day wore on, we got separated enough that I could no longer hear him yelling for Allan. Before I knew it, it was pretty dark. I didn't have a flashlight because I hadn't planned on being out there for that long. I did have the GPS, but the tiny blue screen barely illuminated my feet. It wasn't a full moon, but there was enough light to walk through the dark trees. It was that silvery light that makes everything look like it's moving.

I found myself all but crawling through some old-growth timber. Large trees had fallen over decades ago and rotted away to leave strange hollows where the roots had been and humps where the tree had rotted. The underbrush was thick, and the going was extremely slow, especially in the dark. I knew that if I simply continued toward the moon, I would eventually hit a road, so I wasn't worried. That's when I had a bit of good luck. I saw a faint glimmer of something reflecting moonlight in a way that caught my attention. I had found Allan.

I should clarify. Good luck: I found Allan. Bad luck: I found what was *left* of Allan. Even in the dark, I could tell that he was no longer with us. I'll spare you the worst of the gory details in case of children or sensitive tummies, but his head had been caved in from one side and he was *shredded*. The eye on the left side of his head had popped out of his head, and that's what had caught the moonlight and my attention. (*Yes,* that's sparing the worst of the details.) The slight breeze must've shifted, because I caught a whiff of death and I lost everything I'd eaten that day.

I couldn't have moved Allan if I'd wanted to. He was probably a healthy 180 pounds, so it would've been awkward even if he hadn't been in the dense maze of old growth. I eventually got over my shock and marked the spot on the GPS. I didn't know what had happened to his head, but it seemed obvious that an animal had gotten him. I didn't have many options, so I decided to stay there and watch over him in case the animal came back. I found a good-size stick I could use as a club. I knew it wouldn't do much, but it made me feel better. I used the lighter I always carried to get a small fire going and figured that it would help ward off any animals. I kept the fire very small for safety; burning down the forest wouldn't do anyone any good. In order to protect my night vision, I put my back to the fire and stared into the dark forest.

Thus began my night in the woods with a dead man. I had a watch and used the faint GPS light to keep track of the time. I knew I wasn't getting any sleep, so I started the countdown to dawn. I had found Allan right around midnight, so I had about five hours till light.

Around 3:00, I started hearing louder-than-nighttime noises. The moon was higher, but the shadows were just as thick and seemingly animated. Almost all animals are relatively quiet by nature, either hunting or trying not to be hunted. Whatever was out there was not worried about making noise. At first, I hoped it was David or someone else looking for Allan and/or me. I yelled into the night and the noises immediately stopped. I yelled a few more times without response. I stoked the fire a little and readied my oh-so-deadly stick.

I started screaming in an effort to scare away whatever it was. Most animals avoid humans if possible. Soon enough, the noises returned, but louder and more frenzied. Instead of sounding like something simply crashing through the forest haphazardly, it sounded like something was purposely knocking over trees and thrashing the underbrush. I intensified my screaming and started throwing rocks and sticks toward the noise.

Then a watermelon-sized rock flew over my head and *destroyed* the small tree behind me. I instantly dropped to the ground and shut the F up. I went into panicked silence. That wasn't a little rock! I might have been able to toss it ten feet if I used both hands, but it had been thrown hard enough to demolish a pine tree about five inches in diameter. I inched toward the fire and grabbed the end of a burning stick. I knelt and held the stick above me. I heard a low growl off in the dark. I've heard just about every kind of forest-animal growl—coyotes, wolves, mountain lions, bears, everything. This was something different. It was deeper, more powerful.

My torch seemed to be working, so I grabbed a bigger stick and made a larger torch. The noises slowly subsided and moved off into the night. I'd spent about an hour in my chaotic noise-making match with *something*, and I spent the last hour till the beginnings of dawn constantly swapping torches.

Nothing else happened that night. At first light, I made sure I'd marked the spot with the GPS and headed out for the road. David found me walking back to camp on the road, and I climbed in the truck with him. I told him I'd found Allan and he flipped around to head down the mountain to get help. We'd only gone about a mile when we found a ranger with a radio. He called it in, and the sheriff's department said to wait for them before going back in for Allan. Two deputies were only a few miles off, so it didn't take long before the ranger was using the GPS marker to lead the five of us to where I'd found Allan. One of the deputies had a couple of hound dogs used in search and rescue with him. The closer we got to the spot I'd marked, the more nervous the hounds acted.

Good news: I'd used the GPS correctly and marked the spot. Bad news: Allan wasn't there. In the light, it was obvious that he *had been* there. There was blood everywhere. Again, I'll spare you the gory details, but we did find a couple of *parts* of Allan. After looking around, the deputy with the hounds commented about how there wasn't a drag trail. Whatever had moved Allan was big enough to *pick him up and carry* him through underbrush so thick, it was difficult just to walk through. The dogs were very skittish, but the deputy finally got them to find the trail and we headed off, trailing behind the hounds.

We did finally find most of the rest of Allan, about two miles away. The cause of death was officially ruled a mountain lion attack. None of us who carried Allan out of the woods thought it was a mountain lion. I've helped carry an actual lion-attack victim out of the woods (he lived), and it *did not* match what had happened to

Allan. To this day, there's an area in the mountains above my home-town about five miles in a rough circle that *I will not visit,* even in the daylight.

Dream Demon

SUBMITTED BY JESSICA CALDER

I have always had the ability to see, hear, feel, and communicate with the other side. The veil is very thin for me compared to most, and it has allowed me to grow in a way where I am deeply spiritual and have a mind open to all things otherworldly. I have not, however, always had the knowledge that I do today to keep myself as safe as possible. Experiences like this one have taught me how to do that.

When I was fifteen, I had a best friend (more like a sister) that I did *everything* with. She pretty much lived at my house, and we were inseparable. Let's call her Sarah. Sarah came from a broken, abusive home. She was deeply troubled and found peace and joy in my home and with my family, which is why she was always there. We would take her on vacations with us and everything.

One summer in the late nineties we took her camping. My family *loves* camping! My mom would live in her fifth-wheel trailer parked at a campground if my dad would let her. Because it would have been kind of awkward having a friend sleep in the trailer with me and my parents, we always got to stay in a tent outside. It was so much fun! We would hike, fish, play games, roast s'mores, tell camp-fire stories, and explore the woods around us.

On this particular camping trip, though, Sarah was having a really hard time enjoying herself. Her home life had gotten so bad that she had contemplated suicide. Thankfully, she never followed through on it. Instead of wallowing in misery, she turned to witch-craft for some solace and a sense of control over her world.

Growing up *very* religious, I thought witchcraft was just some-thing you saw in movies. I had no idea that real-world people were into that sort of thing, so it was kind of exciting to see a new side of life. I felt wrong doing it, but I wanted to support my friend.

One night, a very dark and stormy night actually, we had just finished cleaning up the campsite to get everything in out of the rain. We were hunkered down in our tent, shivering, just listening to the thunder, rain, and sounds of the forest.

Sarah turned to me and asked, "Have you ever played with a Ouija board before?"

I said, "No. What's that?" and she grinned menacingly at me.

She got her flashlight, turned it on, placed it halfway under her chin to illuminate her face (like you would when you're telling scary ghost stories), and proceeded to tell me all about how she had been communicating with the dead.

I was fascinated! I had seen spirits all my life, but it was always on their terms and their time. I was so excited to finally be able to communicate with them when and how I wanted!

She didn't have a Ouija board with her, so she went to the camp-site, grabbed an old smelly box (that we kept firewood in), ripped the lid off, grabbed a marker out of our art/activity box (my mom thought we were still little kids, apparently), and made a makeshift Ouija board. For the planchette—the little heart-shaped piece that usually comes with the Ouija—we just used a hair clip, because it was about the same height and size.

She told me to place my fingers on the planchette across from hers and ask a question to the spirits, so I did. Thinking nothing would happen, I kind of sighed, but humored her all the same.

I asked, "Are there any spirits here in the forest that would like to communicate with me?" Just then, the planchette started to move! Of course I thought Sarah was moving it, but she swore up and down it wasn't her.

The planchette moved slowly over to the "yes" circle at the top of the board. I freaked out a little bit but was also very intrigued, so I asked more questions.

"Are you a man or a woman?" MAN

"Do you live in this forest?" YES

"Are you the only spirit here right now?" NO

"Can we speak to the other spirits?" NO

"Why not?" ONLY ME

"Who are you?" DREAM

"What do you mean, 'dream'?" I MAKE DREAMS

"So you put dreams in my head while I sleep?" YES

"I don't believe you. If you really make dreams, what did I dream about last night?" DEATH

I gulped, yanked back my hands, and told Sarah I didn't want to play anymore. Whoever I was communicating with knew *exactly* what I had dreamed the previous night! I'd had a dream that one of my other friend's dads was killed in a horrific motorcycle accident. I'd seen every gory detail until I was scared awake and screaming.

Sarah told me that you can't just stop playing with a Ouija board. You must "close the session," or the spirits can attach themselves to you. I didn't care. I was freaking out and told her I was not playing anymore, and I rolled over to go to sleep. I don't know how, but I eventually fell into a deep slumber with the raindrops tapping our tent as a backdrop to my dream. Or should I say . . . nightmare.

That night, I dreamed about the motorcycle accident once more. This time, there was a black shadow standing next to me on the road. I was stuck! I couldn't move off the road in my dream, and the black shadow just kept cackling at me with a gravelly, throat-phlegmy bellow.

I could hear the motorcycle getting closer and closer. The rumble of the engine hit me before anything else. It shook the ground beneath me. Then, from around the bend in the road, my friend's dad made his debut.

I kept begging the shadow man to let me wake up. I didn't want to see the crash again! I didn't want to watch as he hit a slick spot on the road and flew over the handlebars of his motorcycle, his body impacting the road, the sounds of his torment as he scraped his skin on the asphalt and the ear-piercing, terrified scream of him careening off the cliff, being shredded to pieces with every rock he hit on the way down. I didn't want to hear the breaking of his bones, the metal of his bike twisting and leaving gash marks all over the road, or the cars screeching to a stop behind it all. But most of all, I didn't want to hear the silence that followed.

The shadow man just kept cackling as I was forced to relive this nightmare once more. When it was all over, he twisted his head and craned his neck unnaturally, only mere inches from my face. With his foul breath, he screamed, *"Did I not tell you that I create, control, and manifest your dreams? Do you believe me now?"*

And with that, he faded away like mist and I jolted upright out of bed. It was still dark and raining outside, so I knew it was still night.

I rolled over and shook Sarah awake and told her what had just happened. She chortled and said, "I told you. You didn't close out the game, and now that spirit has attached itself to you."

I begged her to get up and finish the game with me so I could evict this leech from my psyche. She rolled her eyes but complied with my wishes.

We once again placed our hands on the planchette and started asking questions. This time, though, there was no movement, no response, and no closure.

After about an hour, we decided to go back to sleep, so we closed the game and told the spirit he was no longer welcome around us.

I had some very odd, scary, and weird-ass dreams that night, but nothing as terrifying as the accident. I didn't see the dream demon again, either.

The rain was still unrelenting the following day, so we stayed in the trailer playing games, watching movies, and eating junk food all day. That night, however, we both knew what was going to happen.

When we got back to our tent and were sure my parents were asleep, we pulled out that makeshift Ouija board and started hunting for the dream demon. We had a few other spirits come through, but nothing noteworthy. As we were about to give up and go to bed, the planchette started to move on its own! It was one of the creepiest things I've seen. We were both frozen in fear, our eyes unblinking as we watched this thing move around the board, spelling out D. R. E. A. M.

He was back! Once it stopped moving, we quickly placed our fingers on it and started asking questions. We were spitting over our words, trying to ask as many things as we could think of. All to no avail. He didn't answer one single question.

I got so mad that I picked up the board and ripped it in half. I told Sarah that I was never playing with another Ouija board again in my life. She just looked up at me with a level of fear that I had never seen in another person's eyes before.

She said, "Jessica! What did you do?! Now you'll NEVER be able to get rid of him! You've screwed yourself royally, you idiot!"

I replied with some snide remark like, "Yeah, sure I did. That game was dumb, and it was just *you* moving it the whole time anyway."

She then reminded me about the recurring dream and the shadow man I'd seen. I told her that it was just a bad dream because I was scared. She told me to be aware of what my dreams were, because he was real, and he was attached to me forever now.

Now remember: I have the ability to see, hear, and communicate with spirits without a Ouija board. It's just not on my time. I figured that if something did attach itself to me, I would know, because I would be able to feel, see, and hear it.

What I didn't realize at the time was that I had only ever interacted with deceased people—people who had lived, died, and not moved on. This "shadow man" was a whole new breed of shitstorm that I had, up until this point, never known before.

The next morning, we woke up early. The rain had stopped, and we were freezing. My parents were already awake, making breakfast and starting a fire. It was our last day at the campsite, so they wanted to help us pack up the tent after we ate. I was freaking out on the inside, because we'd been dumb enough to just let the ripped-up Ouija board sit in a heap, face up on the side of our tent!

My parents would *kill me* if they knew I had even thought about doing something like that, and they would have banned me from ever hanging out with Sarah again! I couldn't have that, so I had Sarah distract them by trying to show them some "deer she had seen." They both walked down the road a bit to look at the "deer" that obviously weren't there.

When I tell you that I moved faster than a ninja on crack to grab that board and burn it to hell, I mean the world around me was in slow motion! I buried that board under the logs and watched it burn itself to hell! While it was burning (and I was pretending to roast a s'more because my parents were walking back), I had the most chilling sensation tingle up my spine. It felt as though someone were tracing my spine with a fingernail, but ever so gently that you would question whether you'd really felt anything at all. I whipped my head around, but no one was there. I shook it off and went about my life as normal.

When I saw my other friend (we'll call her Melanie) later that week, I told her about the dream I'd had about her dad. She laughed it off, but I could tell she was worried, because I also told her about the dream demon and Ouija board experiences I'd had.

Melanie's dad lived in Las Vegas and would ride his motorcycle up to see her every other weekend. There's one spot he has to bike through to get here that is *extremely* dangerous. Think of a mini Grand Canyon with giant mountains surrounding it. Now picture two poorly maintained narrow roads winding around in sharp curves with zero visibility around the next bend and steep cliffs on either side of you. It is a *dangerous* place to drive. It's called The Gorge, and people wreck, get maimed, and die there all the time. My brother is a life flight pilot and picks people up from The Gorge two or three times a month.

Well, the week I told Melanie was the same week her dad normally came to see her. I tried to reassure her that it was just a stupid dream and Sarah and I were just being dumb in the woods trying to scare each other. Melanie seemed comforted by that and returned to her jovial self in no time.

This was a friend who I didn't live close to or see that often (and this was in the '90s, so cell phones weren't a thing yet), so when I hadn't seen her for almost two weeks, I thought nothing of it. Then my parents told me the news.

They didn't give me any details, but they explained to me that Melanie had moved away to live with her grandma for a while. Her mom wasn't really in the picture. That's when they told me that it all happened so suddenly after her dad had died.

EXCUSE ME? WHAT DID YOU JUST SAY TO ME??

My parents were confused. They thought I already knew everything and were shocked that I had just found out.

I asked them for every single detail. They told me that nearly two weeks before, Melanie's dad was driving his motorcycle pretty fast through The Gorge, and he slipped on a bad patch of road and crashed and died.

I felt like my heart stopped. I'm pretty sure I went into a trance for a few seconds. Every noise was muffled, everything around me was blurry, my body was tingling, and I couldn't comprehend what I had just heard! Amid this shock, I heard a faint "I manifest dreams," followed by deep guttural unnatural laughter. That snapped me right out of it, and I started crying, asking for details and asking about my friend. My parents didn't know anything other than what they had just told me—but *I* did.

I didn't want to believe it, but the dream demon hadn't given me a nightmare: he had given me a front-row seat to a manifested malicious murder of his own design! I ran to my room, screamed into my pillow, and told him to leave me alone and never return!

The sad truth about all this, though, is that I never saw Melanie again. I can't even remember her name, which is why I've come up with that pseudonym. Everything about her, save for the few details I have written here, has been erased from my mind.

The dream demon has never left me. I can usually banish demons with ease. But this parasite has his claws so deep into my subconscious that I cannot remove him. I fear that ripping up and burning that Ouija board sealed my fate and permanently attached him to me.

But it's not all bad. We have a somewhat symbiotic relationship now. I use his "gift" to help me see things in advance, and he uses my life force to stay in this world.

Before that fateful night when he leeched onto me, I only remembered one dream that I repeatedly had as a child. Since that night, however, I can remember *every single dream that I have*. I remember them in such vivid detail that it's almost as if I'm living another life while I sleep in this one.

So, the morals of this story are 1) Never play with Ouija boards, and 2) Check on your loved ones and friends regularly. You never know how you may affect a life simply by being in it.

Sarah and I lost touch over the years after she moved to Vegas at the end of that summer. Oh, how I wish I had listened to her and just finished the damn game.

That's Not My Child

SUBMITTED BY ASHLEY

For as long as I can remember, I've always believed in spirits and things that couldn't be explained. Since childhood, I have heard or seen things happen around my house, but I've never gotten scared by any of it. I have four kids and don't want to freak them out, so I've never told them about any of what I've seen—until my son started seeing things himself.

One day, my oldest son told me about things he would experience in his room—from water bottles falling to the floor (and no, they were not on the edge of his nightstand, nor were there any open windows or fans that could've blown them to the floor), to his closet door opening on its own. Every time he would experience anything new, he would tell me about it, and I would do the same with him. It became our "thing." Luckily, he was never scared, as neither of us was ever hurt, but we still made sure not to mention anything to his older sister or younger brothers. However, one day I did tell my son about an experience I'd had that did freak him out . . . let's just say I did not get much sleep on that creepy night.

We were living in the country at the time, and we rarely got visitors, because everyone complained it was too far away. That was a plus for me, because I don't really like company anyway. On this particular night, I was home alone. All my kids were spending the weekend with grandparents. We were staying in a double-wide trailer at this time, and my room was on one end, with French doors connecting to the master bathroom. When those doors were open, a giant wall mirror made it possible to see the dining room and kitchen (which had a small island), as well as the living room, while I was lying in bed. This was really convenient, because it meant I could keep an eye on my kids whenever they were in there.

Since I was home alone on this night, the only light on was a light above the sink. I had the TV in my room off since I was just lying in bed playing games on my phone. As I was lying in bed, I happened to look up into the mirror. Walking toward my room was the image of a child. I just kept staring at the mirror, watching to see what the child was going to do. When it made it closer to my door, I sat up in my bed. It was then that I realized this image looked identical to my second-youngest child, who was seven years old. The haircut. The complexion. The facial features. The build. Just every-thing. I knew there was no way this could be my son, because he was at his grandma's house with his younger brother.

As soon as I sat up, the image began slowly backing up until it finally disappeared around the kitchen island. I immediately got up and turned on my bedroom light and made my way to the dining room, turning on those lights as well. I looked around the island, and nothing was there. This scared the shit out of me. I quickly grabbed my phone and called my son. I've never been more relieved in my life to hear "Hey, Mama" than I was when he answered his phone.

I don't know what that image was or why it took the shape of my son, but I'm just thankful that my son was safe and sound.

Glimpse into the Future

SUBMITTED BY KATIE

First, a little background info. There is a story we tell in our family, about the youngest daughter of the youngest daughter having abilities with intuition. My grandma always knew things before they happened, my mom as well, and it happens to me often. It's nothing insane for me: just a gut feeling, or a simple dream—but it happens. It could be as simple as a friend stopping by after I got a feeling that it would happen, or a dream about winning a prize and then winning one. It's something that happens to all of us frequently, even if on different levels, and is well known in our family.

On this particular day, I told my mother that my stomach was really upset. I chalked it up to having a meeting that I was a little nervous about. She asked me to reschedule the meeting, since she thought what I was experiencing was one of these "bad feelings" and just wanted me to be safe rather than sorry. But I could not reschedule the meeting because it was an important one at work, so I told myself it was just a nervous stomachache and went on with my day.

I was driving on the interstate. It wasn't super busy, so there was plenty of space to pass other vehicles, and traffic was flowing smoothly. There was a semi-truck in front of me, about five car lengths, and a black truck following closely behind it. I switched lanes to get ready to pass them. All of a sudden it started pouring rain. It had just been sunny and clear, and then it immediately switched to very heavy rain, so thick you could barely see. I didn't think anything of it—this was Indiana, and the weather is unpredictable.

The next thing I knew, the semi-truck began to jackknife, trying to stop, skidding across the pavement. The black truck slammed into it—hard. I reacted quickly, veering onto the shoulder, putting on my brakes to avoid slamming into the accident. Other cars that were farther behind us did the same, leaving traffic at a standstill behind us. I was shaking, feeling like I was about to puke from coming so close to being in an accident. I jumped out of my car to attempt to help the people in the semi and the truck. Rain poured down on me, but it was beginning to lighten up. As I exited my vehicle, I looked toward the accident. The person in the black truck was moving. I told myself that was a good sign, but I couldn't see the driver of the semi-truck. I reached back to slam my car door shut, and then I took my first steps toward the accident.

At the exact moment that I slammed my car door, the scene reset. It wasn't raining. There was no water on the road. In fact, mere seconds had passed since I'd seen the semi-truck five car lengths ahead and prepared to pass it. The semi was back in its lane driving normally, with the black truck following closely. But I was still standing outside my car pulled over on the shoulder, and my body was still shaking from the adrenaline of almost being in an accident. An accident that apparently never happened. I was so confused. I ran my fingers through my hair, a nervous habit of mine, and realized it was soaking wet. I looked at my car and noticed it was covered with water droplets, like it had been through a storm. But there were no other signs of rain. The traffic continued to rush by.

I called my mom to tell her what had happened and obviously canceled that work meeting.

I drive by that spot on occasion, but never if it's raining—just in case.

Ghost Admirer

Submitted by Anonymous

When I was fifteen years old, weird things began to happen around me.

It all started one day when I felt this presence in my room. It wasn't angelic, but it didn't feel demonic, so I kind of wrote it off. And before you ask, yes—I know how angels and demons feel (I can tell you many stories).

The more I felt the presence as weeks went on, certain things stood out to me: it felt male and young, around my age, and neutral. I told my friends about it, and whenever something weird happened, they would joke about it being my "ghost boyfriend," but I would just laugh it off. The name "Ben" stood out to me, so that's what I called him.

Now I should probably tell you that my parents are pastors, and anything not angelic is not welcomed in our house, so I knew better than to just let spirits that don't belong linger. The thing is, Ben never felt harmful to me. But of course I never mentioned anything to my parents, and he never did anything around them. Actually, he never left my room while I was home. That should have been my first warning, as he stayed far away from my parents. But he never did anything to me, so I just let him be.

Apart from things not being where I'd left them or never feeling alone, the freakiest thing that happened was feeling someone sit on my bed some nights. Other people were not so lucky. Anyone who said something insulting about me at school met with an "accident." Nothing horrifying—they would just trip out of nowhere or something random like that. It was funny until it escalated to friends as well. One time, a friend said I should "keep my creepy ghost friend away from them" while taking something out of the trunk of a car, and I literally had to catch the trunk lid before it came down on her head. Another time, my friend Mary was saying how stupid we were to believe that Ben was real and that she didn't believe in any ghosts. She tripped on the stairs as she finished saying that. My other friend and I, who were in front of her a little farther down the stairs, had to catch her so she wouldn't fall. Mary was freaked out for the rest of the day, because she said it felt like someone had pushed her from behind, but we were the only ones on the stairs at the time. A lot of the things that happened did not happen at home. He followed me everywhere—except for church. Still, if anything happened to the people around me, I would tell Ben to leave them alone, and they never had any issues again. But for some dumb reason I never made him leave *me*.

It all came to a head one day while I was in my room listening to the radio and dancing. Ben was kind of like white noise for me most of the time; I felt him in the corner of my mind, but I was good at ignoring him. But this time, I suddenly felt him behind me—I felt breath on the back of my neck. I had goosebumps the size of eggs on my arms. The most ominous feeling came over me. This was the first time I actually *physically* felt him, other than the few times I'd felt the bed dip as though someone had just sat on it. My heart was beating out of my chest, and it was the first time in the six months he was around that I felt scared. I just had this gut feeling that if I brushed it off again, it would only get worse. For some reason I just *knew* deep in myself that I had to face him physically. So I turned around, despite my fear that I might actually see a physical being there. I didn't see anything—but I knew he was there and I was "face to face" with him. I said, as firmly as I could, "You have to leave. You're not welcome here anymore."

I'm from the Caribbean; we don't get cold breezes in summer. But a breeze, like out of a freezer, blew past me, and toward my closed bedroom door. I never felt Ben again. The only person I told about what happened in my room was my sister—definitely never my parents.

In hindsight, I should have cast him out the moment I first felt him, but teenagers can be dumb sometimes.

My Mother's Alien Encounter

SUBMITTED BY SELENA

I'll start with my mom. She is a diabetic, and before this event she was in and out of the hospital for diabetes-related problems. I almost lost her a few times. Because of that, I felt like I needed to watch over her, and I became sensitive to how she felt at any given time.

One night, I woke up to hear her screaming and praying in her sleep. Our rooms were next to each other, so it wasn't hard to hear her. I ran into her room, glancing at the time as I went—it was 4:43 a.m.

When I walked through the door, I noticed that it was bright. Like middle-of-the-day, sun-coming-in-through-the-windows bright. Which made absolutely no sense, because for the seven years that we lived in that apartment, she always had foil paper on her windows to keep the sun from coming in *and* blackout curtains on top of that. Not to mention that Daylight Saving Time hadn't even happened yet that year, so at that time the sun didn't come up until around seven where we were. But in that moment, I had just woken up and run to her without even thinking about it.

I woke her up, and her face immediately let me know that she was terrified. She told me she had been having an ugly dream and that she was still scared. So, without asking, I crawled into her bed so I could keep an eye on her. As we were still lying there, half-awake and half-asleep, bright yellow and orange light started filling up the room. She turned to me and said she wasn't sure if she was still dreaming, but something was standing right next to her, wearing a purple skin-tight uniform. I looked over and didn't see a thing, but I got a very, very eerie feeling that I realized was coming from a corner of the room. I couldn't put my finger on it and, although I was very scared, I was also very sleepy, and as much as I tried to fight it, I fell asleep holding on to my mom.

The next day, neither of us mentioned it—not out of shock but because we'd almost forgotten what had happened. Later on that same day, I asked my mom what had been going on the previous night. She told me about the figure in the purple uniform with almond-shaped, blacked-out eyes hovering over her and told me, "But I was awake. I was looking at it." I agreed, saying, "I was also scared even though there was light."

Right then, it clicked for both of us: there was never any light in my mother's room. It wasn't even five in the morning. She had blackout curtains on the windows. That's when we got into detail about everything. The big head, with those big eyes and a metallic skin-tight purple suit with those shoulder pads that stick out. Big hands, and a skin tone that ranged from tan like our skin to gray.

After that, nothing similar ever happened again, but my mother never really got sick again, either. To this day, we think it had a lot to do with that alien encounter somehow.

Inside My Mirror

SUBMITTED BY ANONYMOUS

In 2018, I moved into a two-bedroom rental with a friend of mine. I have since moved out of this house. But in that place, my bed was in the middle of the room, with the head of the bed sitting against the back wall. To the right of the bed was a window, and a built-in wardrobe stood against the wall to the left. Two sliding doors on the wardrobe were both covered with mirrors. My bed was incredibly close to these mirrors. Unfortunately, there wasn't any way for my bed to be positioned in the room without the mirror reflecting it, but at that time I had never heard of it being bad to sleep with a mirror facing you, so I didn't think anything of it.

I was home by myself, and it was somewhere between midnight and 4:00 a.m. I was in my bedroom with my lights on, lying on my bed and texting with a friend. I caught a glimpse of movement in the mirror and looked over. In the reflection, some sort of bugs were crawling around under my bed. I freaked out and stuck my head over the edge of the bed, searching the floor and under my bed. There was no sign of any bugs or movement. I looked directly up into the mirror and could still see the bugs! There they were, right there in front of me, but only in the mirror. I thought I was going crazy. I'd never experienced hallucinations like this before, and have never experienced any like them since. But it gets weirder.

I texted my friend, telling them about what was happening and how there were bugs in my mirror but not actually in my room, kind of trying to laugh it off, but also freaking out and feeling super scared. For about twenty minutes, I stepped in and out of my bedroom, looking in the mirror and then immediately under my bed. I tried moving boxes around under my bed and then watched myself in the reflection to guide my way to these bugs. And no matter how closely I looked in the mirror, I couldn't identify what bugs they were. I live in Australia and we have lots of crazy insects, so I can easily recognize cockroaches, different spiders, moths, beetles, and more. The bugs in the mirror looked like a weird mix of a cockroach and a spider, skittering around with a long body and multiple long legs.

After repeating the cycle of trying to see these bugs in real life, I gave up and turned off all my lights—except for a small bedside light—and tried to go to sleep. But a few minutes later, I saw more movement in the mirror from the corner of my eye, *much* bigger than the bugs this time. It was a dark cloaked figure, as tall as my ceiling, looming in the mirror's surface. I felt terrified, a kind of fear I've never felt before. The figure started to move out of my mirror, and it was directly in front of me, in real freaking life, at the end of my bed. I panicked. I frantically turned my lamp on, but the figure stayed. I flicked it on and off again, and when it turned off, the figure started to move toward me. I remember screaming, and squeezing my eyes closed and opening them again, but it stayed, still slowly creeping toward me. Genuinely fearing for my life, I decided to scream *at* it. I screamed for it to stop. To go away. Loudly. Over and over. And just like that, it vanished.

It's safe to say that I didn't sleep after that, and I continuously checked my mirror for the next few months. I never experienced anything like that again, and in 2019 moved into a different home with my partner. In my new bedroom, there is a built-in wardrobe with three doors, but thankfully only one is mirrored. Still, I've made it my damn routine since day one to move the doors at bedtime and always ensure that the mirror is *never* reflecting the bed.

She Fixed Me

SUBMITTED BY ASHLEY

The night of August 2, 2014, I was given the worst news in the world: my best friend had just passed away. I felt like part of my soul died right then. She and I would joke about how we were soulmates and when we got old we would be on our deathbeds together. This killed me. I was crying so hard. My four-year-old sleepwalked out of her room, hugged me, and went right back to bed—but I felt like I just couldn't stop.

Fast-forward to November 2014. My period was late. At first I didn't think much of it, but for fun I looked up what my due date would be if I were to have gotten pregnant: August 2, 2015—my best friend's birthday and death day. I knew right then that I was pregnant. I went out and bought a test kit and it confirmed what I already felt: that the universe was giving me a gift. I had experienced such a loss, but now I would be getting such a blessing.

But in December of that year, I found out that my baby was not viable and I would miscarry. It was like some sick joke. I was so angry and depressed. I didn't miscarry on my own until January 15, 2015. I was devastated. For the rest of 2015, all of 2016, and most of 2017 I was in a terrible mental state. Panic attacks, depression—it was not a good place to be.

In July 2017, just before my birthday, I decided to go to an astrologer. I heard they were really good at understanding your life, and

I wanted to ask about when I would get pregnant again. The appointment was life-changing. The astrologer told me that my window, according to astrology, showed that I wouldn't be able to carry a baby from 2011 all the way to September 2017! I was *shocked!* I'd had my first daughter in February 2011. He told me she had been destined to be born at that time—if she hadn't, she wouldn't have been until 2017.

Now, my husband and I had quit trying because I was just too emotionally drained. But on October 3, 2017, I started spotting, and then it was gone. I waited a couple of days and then decided to test. It was negative. I went to throw the test into the garbage, but at the last second I thought to take it to the window, figuring that in the sunlight maybe it would show a slight line. It did! So I went out and bought a couple more tests, trying one later in the day and then another the next morning. All were positive. But I didn't allow myself to get excited until I saw this baby on an ultrasound—I was that cautious after all I had been through.

At nine weeks, my friend took me to my ultrasound appointment. I told her she was not allowed to be excited, because I was worried the pregnancy could end badly. She was sitting where she could see the screen and I couldn't yet. I watched her face—and I saw happy tears. Then I looked, and there was my baby. My baby girl. She was born June 18, 2018.

This story is not done yet. In 2019, I went to deliver some product. I sold Norwex cleaning products at the time. This older lady I was delivering to invited me in to see her crystals. We sat down to chat and she said she was a medium, someone who could speak to spirits. And she told me that my best friend was around. She asked about my miscarriage. The medium said, "That was your friend. She needed to fix something so you could carry *this* baby to term." In that moment, I felt healed. My heart healed. It made so much sense.

With my first daughter, my body didn't go into labor; my daughter and I both almost lost our lives and I had an emergency C-section. Having my second was easy. Easy pregnancy. Easy, natural, and beautiful labor.

Today, my daughters and I are so happy and healthy, and I feel blessed that my best friend is watching over me from the other side.

A Tall Slender Figure

SUBMITTED BY AUDREY

In 2017, my husband and I moved into our first apartment together. We lived on the second floor of our building, and each level had three apartments. And on each floor, there was a porch light between all three apartments, so that the area by all the doors was lit at all times. We had no control over this light and it could never be turned off. The apartment had blinds, already provided by the building, but the light would still shine into our bedroom.

When we first moved in, our room was set up like this: We had the bed up against the wall away from the door, so the window was on the right. Down a small hallway and to the left, there was a bathroom. If you left the door open to the bathroom, it showed right into the vanity mirror.

Every night, I slept on the left side of the bed. We hadn't gotten curtains yet, so I would lie facing the left side of the room so the bright porch light outside didn't shine in my face. My husband usually slept facing me, since he could also avoid the light at that angle.

One very normal night a couple of months into living in this place, we got into bed. I was lying there, trying to fall asleep. My husband had used the bathroom and left the door open, so I could see the window behind me in the mirror. I was kind of in and out, shutting and opening my eyes trying to fall asleep, when all of a sudden I saw a tall, slender figure, completely in black, behind me in the mirror. It was outlined perfectly, looking kind of like Slender Man in the light. I remember closing my eyes shut super-tight and going back to sleep. I assumed it was a dream and tried not to think much about it.

After that, I always made sure the bathroom door was shut. Eventually, I asked my husband if we could move the furniture around so that I couldn't see the bathroom or mirror anymore.

I didn't tell anyone about this happening, but months later, my husband's stepbrother came to stay with us for the weekend, and they were drinking. My husband likes to tell crazy stories when he drinks, and he started telling his brother about the alien he killed in our apartment. All the color went out of my face, and I asked him what he was talking about. He was shocked that I didn't know.

His story was basically the same as mine—but, instead of my closing my eyes and going back to sleep as had actually happened, in his story I turned over and screamed because there was an alien standing right next to the bed. The best way I can describe it is what people call "the grays." Kind of reminiscent of the Kaminoins from *Star Wars*: tall and skinny humanoids with gray skin, no hair, and very large dark eyes.

My husband's story continued: he said he jumped out of the bed and ran to turn on the light in the room, when the figure disappeared. He then got tackled by something—he realized he had to turn off the light to see whatever this thing was. He turned the light off again, and it was right in front of him on the other side of the room. Then he grabbed it, punched it, and started strangling it. At that point, he said he remembers feeling its neck break under his hands, and suddenly he was waking up in the bed next to me and it was morning.

I had never talked to him about what I had seen, and this was the first time I was hearing his version of the events. We have never had another experience like that one, and we still talk about it to this day.

Dog's Day to Die

SUBMITTED BY GEMGEMS

This all happened on January 12, 2023. I was watching YouTube with my healthy dog on my lap. My friends called me and wanted to meet up at the pool, since it was perfect summer swimming weather here in Australia. I got there first and swam around for a while before my friends showed up. A few hours later, they left, and it was just me and a few other people. I remember one of the lifeguards coming up to me and telling me that the pool was closing soon, so I should start packing up my stuff.

The only people left at the pool at that time were an older couple who were just leaving, a mom and her four kids, two teenage boys, and of course me and the lifeguards. I left the pool and started to drive back home.

When I arrived home, my dog was lying dead on the floor. I was shocked and started crying for what felt like hours. By the time I had pulled myself together enough to bury her and figure out how she had died, it was dark outside. That's when I realized that there was no clear indication of what had happened. I just brushed it off as old age, or maybe she had been sick without showing any symptoms, or maybe she had eaten something she shouldn't have. I went to bed, too sad to do anything more, and cried myself to sleep.

When I opened my eyes, I was in the pool again. I was in my bathing suit and it was the morning. My friends had only just arrived and jumped into the pool exactly how I remembered it happening before I'd fallen asleep. My first thought was that this was a lucid dream.

That's when I remembered my dog, and I got out of the pool, quickly getting ready to drive home, saying a quick goodbye to my friends. When I got home, I saw my dog about to take a drink of water. And that's when I saw it: a cane toad floating around in the water! Cane toads are really poisonous frogs that can kill other animals—and definitely small dogs who drink water where they've been swimming. We have a lot of them where I live in Australia. I stopped my dog before she could take a drink and put the toad in a jar, setting it down on the kitchen table.

That's when I woke up again, to my healthy dog licking my face. To say that I was confused is an understatement. I was in bed. It was morning, and I was still in my bathing suit because I had been too sad to change before bed the previous night. That's when I remembered the cane toad. I jumped out of bed and bolted to the kitchen. There was a cane toad in a jar sitting on the table.

Fast-forward to about five years later, and my friends and I still have no idea what happened on that day. They say they don't even remember my leaving early, but they do remember going to the pool with me that day, which rules out the "it was a dream in a dream" theory.

My family thinks it might have been a dream, but that doesn't explain the cane toad on the table when I woke up, or my dog dying and rising from the dead after I had buried her obviously dead body. I guess it just wasn't my dog's day to die.

A LOOK
OF HORROR

Two Moms

This happened in the early 2000s. My husband, our children, and I were living in a suburb of Chicago. It was mid-afternoon on a weekday, so I was getting ready for work. I stepped out of the shower, and I could hear my seven-year-old daughter speaking to someone. At first I didn't think anything of it, because I thought she was talking to my son, who shared a room with her. I walked out of the bathroom and realized I could hear my daughter crying while still carrying on a conversation. My mom brain kicked in, and I immediately headed into her room to see what was going on.

My daughter was on the top of her bunk bed, with her eyes fixed across the room where her dresser was. I then realized she was begging and pleading . . . with me. I heard her saying "Mommy, Mommy! Why won't you talk to me?? Mommy, *please talk to me!!*" Only I was standing in her doorway looking up at her. My daughter was *sobbing*. I called her name, and her head whipped around. She looked at me, and at that moment you could see every last bit of blood leave her face. She had a look of straight horror. She stared back at the dresser, then back at me, then back to the dresser—and then leaped from the top of the bunk bed into my arms. She hugged me so tight and said that I had walked into the room, woken her up from her nap when I turned the light on, gone to her dresser, and begun getting ready for work. She said she tried talking to me, but I wouldn't answer her or turn around. When she heard me call her, the "me" at the dresser disappeared. I held onto her so tight. I took her with me to my room, got dressed, and we got the hell out of there.

My daughter is now twenty-nine years old, with her own family. When we have get-togethers, we still talk about what happened.

Glitch at the Crematorium

SUBMITTED BY ROSIE

I used to work in a crematorium in South Wales in the UK. Even though I was surrounded by death, I never believed in spirits or ghosts—until this happened.

One night at work, I was sitting with my boss in her office. There are big TV screens on the wall in there, showing a continuous video feed from the cameras in the building. In the middle of our conversation, my boss stopped talking when she saw one of my colleagues, John, on the video feed climbing a ladder over the crematory machines. She pointed it out and I turned around to look too, shocked to see him do that. We've had a lot of training and are told never to go up there, especially alone, because of how dangerous it is.

We both got up and went next door to the big warehouse where the machines and morgue are, intending to figure out exactly what John was doing, but he was nowhere to be seen. We started yelling up to him to come down, but he didn't reply. Fearing that he might have fallen down the side of the 800°C ovens, we started to panic. We called his mobile phone, and he answered. My boss shouted at him, telling him to get down from the ladder and that he had us all worried. She asked why he hadn't responded to us when we shouted at him to come down.

Confused, John said he wasn't even working that day and had been home the whole time. My boss's face went pale, and we ran back to the office to check the security camera. Even though we both had seen him climbing up that ladder, it hadn't been picked up on the recording; to this day, neither of us can explain what happened.

I Felt Myself Die

SUBMITTED BY VALERIE

Here's my glitch-in-the-matrix story: I heard, saw, and felt myself die.

It was 12:00 a.m. on November 4, 2015. I was thirty-eight weeks pregnant with my first child, and my husband drove me to the hospital to get induced because I had preeclampsia. Once I was in a delivery room, the nurses set up my IV and started giving me Pitocin to help my body start labor. Two hours passed and my water sac broke. I could feel my son moving. My husband called the nurse. She checked to see if I was dilated and found that I was only two centimeters, so I still had a while to go. She said, "I'll give you ten minutes, and I'll come check on you again."

Five minutes passed with my son kicking like hell in my stomach and me screaming in pain. My husband called the nurse. I was still at 2 centimeters. She hit an alarm, and eight standby nurses came in. They started preparing for an emergency C-section, taking me into a second room. I freaked out, begging my husband to call my mother, who he doesn't like. She worked at the McDonald's down the street. But before she could get there, the doctor came in and told me there was no way I could wait—the baby was in distress. They flipped me over, administered an epidural, and not even two minutes later I could feel the doctor cutting into my stomach. The pain was excruciating. My stomach felt like it was on fire. My husband was looking me right in my face telling me everything was going to be okay, but my whole body was shaking. I could feel my doctor digging around in my stomach, and then finally I heard my son let out his first cry. I looked to my husband. The doctor walked toward him with our son.

The alarm on my monitor started going crazy. I could see the doctor toss my son to my husband, and he started requesting blood. More nurses entered the room. The alarm began beeping and beeping over and over. My husband walked toward me with our son. I could see my baby's little fingers, his cute little nose, and then the monitor went silent. A flat-line beep rang across the entire room. Nurses grabbed my son from my husband, who began to scream. One moment I was looking at my husband; and then all of a sudden I could see *me*: my mouth closed, pale white.

I moved across the room to the end of the bed and looked at my stomach, ripped open with blood pooling like a lake under the frame. I stood at the edge of the bed next to my husband. He was holding my foot that was dangling to the side. The doctor came back into the room and said he was sorry. He did everything he could do.

I turned to look at my husband and then the room completely changed around me. Suddenly I was sitting in the first delivery room with the nurse at the end of my bed. My husband was holding my hand. The nurse checked to see how much I was dilated. I was nine centimeters and ready to deliver.

There was a knock at the door. We were expecting it to be the doctor, but my mother ran in, screaming "Is everything okay?!" My husband got really upset and asked her what the hell she was doing in the delivery room, and how she had found us in this particular room. My mother looked at him with a blank face. I'm staring, speechless and freaking out. My mother looked him dead in the face and said, "Troy, what are you talking about? You just called me out of work saying that there was an emergency and that I needed to get here immediately." My husband turned to me and said, "No, I didn't. I've been standing here by Valerie this whole time."

The door opened and my doctor walked in. "All right, every-one—who's ready to deliver a baby?" I vaginally delivered a healthy 6-pound, 5-ounce baby boy without any complications on November 5, 2015. As my doctor laid my son on my chest, I stared mesmerized by my baby's fingers and his cute little nose, looking exactly how he'd looked moments ago when he was cut out of me.

I don't know what happened. I don't know how I jumped from an emergency C-section right back to the moments before everything started turning south. And to this day my mom swears my husband called her at work and told her to come. There was no way she would have known to come, and where we were. We hadn't told anyone where we were going to deliver our son.

I told my mom what had happened, and she said that God knew what he had in store for me—that I wouldn't have had my two other boys if my time hadn't been reset, and that I shouldn't fear this "glitch in the matrix." Instead, I should thank it for giving me a second chance.

Hide-and-Seek

SUBMITTED BY KEO

When I was younger, less than ten years old, my second-oldest sister, who was four years older than me, and I were playing hide-and-seek in the house we grew up in. This home was definitely haunted. I had so many scary experiences and nightmares while living there.

It was my turn to be "it," so my sister went to go hide. I was upstairs looking everywhere, but could not find her, so I decided to check the basement. When I opened the door, I saw her run and hide underneath the staircase. I ran downstairs, yelling "I found you!" But she wasn't there. I was so confused.

I went to the bottom of the staircase and was about to walk back up when I saw her again—but at the top of the stairs this time. I said, "Hey! You were supposed to wait until I found you." Then she ran off again.

When I got back upstairs, I saw her with our oldest sister, drawing. I asked her why she wasn't hiding anymore. She said, "You took too long to find me, so I stopped playing a while ago. I've been in this room drawing."

I told them the story, but they didn't believe me. Then I told my mom, and she said, "Oh, someone in Laos just died and she sort of looks like your sister. Maybe that was her you were playing with." I was freaked out! So I was playing hide-and-seek with a ghost?

I'm turning thirty in a week or so, and I still remember this like it was yesterday. It still gives me the chills, and that house still terrifies me.

Snowy Drive

Submitted by Freya

This is one of several near-death experiences I had while living and working in Yosemite National Park.

One winter evening, my boyfriend and I were returning to the park after a quick trip to a nearby town for groceries, about a ninety-minute drive. As we were coming in on Highway 41, and at the highest elevation, we got caught in heavy snow. We stopped to put on the snow chains, then tried to continue driving, but the snow was coming down so hard that the chains just weren't enough, even at only ten to fifteen miles per hour.

I had been doing the driving up to that point, but I was too scared to keep driving, so I asked my boyfriend to take over. He did, and we tried to continue making our way down the mountain as slowly and carefully as we could. We were both terrified—the car was slipping all over the road, which had at least a thousand-foot drop-off on one side, and no guardrail.

At one point, we started sliding and spinning and lost all control of the vehicle, and we began sliding toward the edge of the drop-off. We were screaming, and both of us thought we were about to die as we grabbed each other and closed our eyes.

The front wheels of my car were hanging over the edge, and then suddenly, out of nowhere, we felt a jerk (or maybe a push) that propelled us backward toward the snowbank on the other side of the road. We hit it with a crash, hard enough that it dented my back bumper.

We opened our eyes and were both so confused about how the car's wheels had gotten back onto the road, let alone how we ended up on the other side. Terrified by the experience, we hugged each other and cried while we waited inside our car for the snow to stop before driving again.

We were the only ones on the road for hours. When we finally got down to the valley, we were so grateful to have made it out alive.

I've been terrified of driving in snow ever since. Not sure if this was a matrix glitch or an angel, but either way . . . it saved our lives.

Wrong Apartment

SUBMITTED BY AMY

I've *never* told anyone this story before, because to this day I still struggle to understand what happened. This is wild, so buckle up.

In 2002, I got a divorce and moved myself and my two children into a small apartment in a four-plex apartment building: two apartments upstairs, and two downstairs. There were four of these four-plexes on this block, but mine was white on the outside and the others were tan. We occupied the top-floor apartment on the left-hand side of the building, directly across the hall from an apartment that belonged to a trusted friend of mine, Dawn. I asked Dawn to watch my kids for me while I went to the grocery store, as my kids were two and four at the time and shopping with toddlers can be difficult. When I got back, I pulled up directly in front of my building, the white one, and I saw my four-year-old son waving at me from my apartment window. I waved back and grabbed the bags and went inside.

I climbed the stairs, opened my door, and immediately realized I was in the wrong apartment. Now, remember, there are only two apartments on a floor, and they're directly across from each other. There's no way I could have walked into one that wasn't mine, as there's only one apartment on the lefthand side. But, it wasn't mine. The furniture wasn't mine, it smelled like men's cologne, there was a big area rug on the floor that wasn't mine—this was *not* my apartment.

I shut the door, grabbed my bags, and went back to my car, thinking I had walked into the wrong building since I had only lived there for a couple of weeks at that point. But no: I sat in my car and saw my son again in the window of *that* building—in the window that would be my living room. I ran back in, without my groceries this time, and flung the door open, thinking I had to save my children; but when I opened the same door I had just wrongfully entered, it was now my apartment.

I was totally confused and must have looked terrified, because my friend asked if something was wrong. I told her I didn't know what had happened and I started to tell her about entering the wrong apartment, but she cut me off and asked why I had been sitting in my car for so long. She said they saw me pull up, my son waved from the window, and then they watched me sit with my hands on the steering wheel for about five solid minutes, staring straight ahead. Then they saw me run out of my car toward the building without the groceries, and she thought something bad had happened because I looked panicked. I tried to tell her that I thought I had gone into the wrong apartment, but she said I just sat in my car, motionless.

I still don't know what happened, and I've never told anyone about this because I didn't want someone to think I was unfit to raise my kids, since my ex and I were going through a custody battle at the time, too. My kids are twenty-four and twenty-two now, so I guess it's safe to share.

Listen to Your Pets

SUBMITTED BY KASSI

This only happened about a week before I am writing this, so I know my memory isn't playing tricks on me. But ever since, I haven't been able to really sleep and I'm looking at different apartments.

For a little background, I live in a small town in British Columbia, Canada, and there are only a few options for apartment buildings—three total, in fact. And one of these buildings barely has residents, due to the supernatural activity that has been witnessed there. I thought people were being overly superstitious and decided to move there after I graduated since the rent was cheap. I have lived in the building for nine months now and I had never witnessed anything weird up until last week.

I was texting my boyfriend while I had a show on for background noise. My boyfriend and I were talking, and my boyfriend sent a specific text that I vividly remember having replied to. I looked up into the hallway where the front door was (I live in a bachelor pad so I could see the door from my bed) and saw my cat seated by the door looking up. He meowed and jumped at the handle, and suddenly there was a knock at the door.

Nobody ever knocks at my door, so I quickly got up and grabbed a small pocket knife from my purse before I went to open it, not knowing what to expect. My cat ran under my bed. When I opened the door, I was suddenly in bed again, opening the exact same text from my boyfriend which showed that I had not replied. When I looked up toward the door, my cat was sitting in the exact same spot, looking at the handle, but this time he didn't meow or jump, and now my TV was off. There was a sudden knock at the door again, and I had an eerie feeling, so I stayed in bed and tried to stay quiet. The knock got aggressive, and then I heard footsteps walk away.

The next day, there was news that a known convict had broken into my apartment building and robbed two apartments. I cannot explain what happened or why, but I fully believe something or someone was looking out for me that night.

I Don't Think That Was My Dad

SUBMITTED BY ALLIE

Okay, so this has to be the weirdest thing that's ever happened to me. I was about seven or eight years old, and I lived in a three-story home with my mom, dad, dog, and twin sister. We had our friends Madison and Summerlyn over for the night. Our dads were close friends and decided to go out to the bar that night and have some fun while we stayed home with my mom. So it was just my sister, mom, Madison, Summerlyn, me, and our dog Jessie.

My mother always went to bed around nine or ten at night, but my sister, our friends, and I stayed up late. Eventually my sister and Summerlyn went to bed, and Madison and I were still awake. At around 1:00 a.m. we heard my dog barking. At first it freaked us out, but then we realized it was going to wake everyone up, so we went to get him.

Everyone's bedrooms were on the second floor, and Jessie, our dog, was downstairs barking. Madison and I walked out of the bedroom to go down the front staircase, which is right in front of my parents' room. As we were walking to get Jessie, my dad walked out of the bedroom. It was dark, so at first his appearance scared me a little. But then I looked at him and, even though he was pale as snow, he was dressed in casual everyday clothes and even had his shoes on—sort of normal. But then I realized that when he had left for the bar, he'd been dressed in completely different clothes and shoes. And again, it's 1:00 a.m.

I said to my dad, "Hey, Jessie is barking."

He looked at me and asked, "Who's Jessie?"

I looked back at him and said, "Our dog Jessie, Dad."

He looked at me again and said, "Who's Jessie?"

At this point, I was scared out of my mind. He was just standing there staring at me with a straight face, not even moving. And I started to wonder: *Why does he have all of his clothes on and why is he pale and why is he asking me who our dog is?*

As I turned around to look at Madison, she wasn't even there. She ran off because she was so scared. So I darted back into my bedroom to find her in the bed also freaking out. We went to bed, even though we were both scared.

When we woke up the next day, I went up to my dad and asked him if he remembered seeing me last night at 1:00 a.m., and I asked him why he said he didn't know who Jessie was. He looked at me and said, "I wasn't even home at 1:00 a.m. I was still at the bar."

I swear to this day it freaks me out, because who was I talking to?!

No Drowning

SUBMITTED BY GORDANA

I didn't learn how to swim until I was about six years old, but my parents let me go into the water on my own, unsupervised and without a flotation device, before then. I know, nuts! But those were different times.

One day I was at the beach playing in water up to my waist, when all of a sudden a big wave took me under the water and dragged me out into the ocean.

Although the wave was unexpected, I managed to hold my breath for a bit. I found myself in the deep water, walking on the bottom of the sea, when all of a sudden I had no more air. Then I remember taking a deep breath as if I was out of the water (it must have been an automatic reflex)—but, to my surprise, I didn't get water in my lungs.

I kept walking, and I kept breathing. It was a few minutes until I resurfaced; and, once on shore, I could not believe that I had breathed normally *under water*!

This is one of my core memories. I don't know how to explain it; it just happened. I guess it was not my day to drown.

Portal in the Hallway

SUBMITTED BY KELLY

About nine months ago, I was at my boyfriend's mom's house. We help take care of her and sleep over every other night. I have been going to this house for three years, and during the Covid lockdown I cared for her during the day, so I am very familiar with this house and its layout.

On this particular night, I walked down the hallway to go to the bathroom. I didn't turn on the hallway light, just the bathroom light. When you walk out of the bathroom, to your left is a closet, followed by a hallway that turns to the left and goes down to the living room. So it's a really quick turn around the corner. Three steps, maybe.

I switched off the bathroom light and proceeded to walk back to the living room where my boyfriend was. I was looking down at my phone. I turned the corner and bumped into a man. We were both startled. When I looked around, I was in a dark alley on a dirt road flanked with candle-lit streetlamps. I looked at the man and got this feeling of "You are not supposed to see me." It was as if he was trying to get away or hide from someone. As soon as I realized this, I was standing back in that hallway.

I told my boyfriend, "I just bumped into a man in the hallway." He nodded and didn't say a thing. He has experienced things there too, but doesn't talk about it.

WEIRD VIBES

What Was in That Closet?

SUBMITTED BY NICHOLE

In the spring of 2004, my friend K and I went to look at a house for rent by its owner; I had found it in a newspaper ad. It was in our hometown, but in an area where we didn't go very often. I drove us there, and the first thing I noticed was that the house had a large driveway and that the side yard connected to a laundromat with an even bigger parking lot. I was in my early twenties and got together with a group of friends every week, so my first thought was *We'd have so much room for parking when we have parties!* (We all lived in houses with street-only parking, so this was a big deal.)

We were a little early, so we sat in the driveway. I always have very detailed memories of significant events in my life, and this was no different, so I can vividly remember both the house we saw and the house to its left, which had a big tree in the front yard and a hole in one of the windows, about the size of a baseball. The distance between that house and the one we went into was maybe six to eight feet. The man showing us the house arrived, and there was nothing unusual or creepy about him. He didn't give off any weird vibes and seemed very average. Just a guy. Probably in his mid-forties, slightly overweight, showing us a house.

The front door of the house faced the street, but he told us to come in through the kitchen. There was a small back porch where only the steps to it, not the kitchen door, were visible from the street.

I noticed random things—the house hadn't been updated since it was built, which was probably in the '40s or '50s (common for that area). It was kind of dirty, and there were built-in bookcases and a boarded-up window in the living room. The man said it was because they built a shed attached to the house. This didn't make sense from what we could see from the driveway, but I didn't think much of it.

We continued through the house, walking a U-shape path (kitchen in the back, then bathroom, rectangular-shaped living room in the front, then down a hall with two bedrooms; the main bedroom was in the back, next to the kitchen), and the man started talking about how we're going to fight over who gets the main bedroom because it had a huge walk-in closet and "I know how you girls are with clothes."

We were laughing about that as we walk into the bedroom. The light wasn't on—I don't think any lights were on in the entire house—and there was a curtain over the window, so while hazy sunlight filtered in, overall the room was pretty dark. He pointed to the closet, which was really just a door frame and pitch-black inside. He told us we should check out the closet, as it goes all the way back a few feet.

At this point, the red flags are waving too hard to ignore. K was standing behind me at an angle where I couldn't see her face, but I felt the tension radiating off of her. I could hear her voice in my head screaming that we needed to leave, but every fiber of my being was telling me that we needed to play it cool to survive. I smiled and said something like, "Oh, I don't have a lot of clothes." (Complete lie.) He tried again. K said something like, "We share clothes." He tried for a third time, and I changed the subject to something else about the house. This went on for probably five minutes: we kept trying to change the subject to get out of that room, and he kept stalling and bringing it back up.

That's the last memory we both have in the house. Then it was like I was watching myself from outside my body. Suddenly, I was in the driver's seat of my car, and we were at a red light a few miles away. K's mouth was moving, but I couldn't hear her. You know that "pop" noise you hear when you come up from underwater? I heard that, and then I could hear her talking again. We were in the middle of an entirely unrelated conversation. I looked at the time on my dash, and it was significantly later. I said this to K, and that I didn't remember leaving the house. She didn't either. It's super weird, but we chalk it up to being in survival mode because we knew something bad would have happened if we'd gone into that closet. To make it seem less crazy than it was, when we saw our friends that night we said, "Hey, guys, wanna hear how we almost died today?" in a joking manner. We neglected to mention that we didn't remember leaving or the missing chunk of time.

A few weeks passed, and we went to meet our friends at a bar just past the house we had seen. As we were driving down the street where we should have seen that house, we noticed that it wasn't there. Like the entire house was just gone, with no possibility of its ever having existed. The house with the broken window was next to the laundromat. There's no way another house with a driveway could have ever fit in that spot. And it couldn't have been demolished, as there were no remnants of a foundation or the driveway, not even the cutout on the curb to the street. The grass was high, like it hadn't been cut in weeks.

Until that moment, we'd thought it was a potential assault or kidnapping situation that we'd managed to get out of. Because we didn't have physical evidence and that kind of stuff wasn't taken as seriously back then, we didn't report it. A few days later, I drove past the house location again to make sure it wasn't a "we were talking and missed it" type situation. But it still wasn't there.

K and I both have had our fair share of paranormal and weird experiences, but nothing like this. It was easier to just deny that house not being there than it was to try to explain it. Years passed before either of us ever told anyone else about what had happened. I have no idea where we went, what was in that closet, or how we got out alive that day. Even now, nearly twenty years later, if I think about it too much, my skin crawls, the hair stands up on the back of my neck, and I feel really uncomfortable.

Mystery Salon

SUBMITTED BY SARAI

I was twenty-two years old in 2013, and I was about to get out of the Navy. I wanted to get my hair done, but did not have anywhere to go since I am not from San Diego. I googled many salons near where I was staying and finally found one that I liked, based on the reviews. I called and made an appointment.

The day of my appointment came. I got myself ready and left. My GPS took me to a salon that had a store inside it (sort of like Ulta). It was run by one lady, which I thought was odd, but she verified my name and appointment, so I just continued. I told her what I wanted done, and she sat me down and began. She then started to ask me some personal questions. The weird thing is that she acted like she knew me. She asked me about my sister, my parents, and my nephews (it was so odd that she knew). She even asked me how my nephew with autism was doing. I am very nonconfrontational, so I just gave her simple answers.

Then these teen kids came into the salon, and she started speaking to spirits, asking them to protect her and the salon from the kids. It was *so odd*, but my hair was still in process, so I just let it go.

She asked me about my husband (then boyfriend) and said we were going to get married and have a beautiful marriage. She also said that it would be a long time before I returned to California. She said I was going to have three kids by the time I came to visit California again.

Finally, she finished. I was relieved that I was able to leave, because I was so nervous and scared.

I made it back to where I was staying and noticed that I had a missed call and had gotten a voicemail from the salon I had made the appointment with. The voicemail said that they were wondering where I was, because I had not shown up for my appointment. I freaked out!

A few days later, I went back to the salon I had visited, but I *couldn't find it anywhere!* It was completely gone, like it never had existed. I really thought I was going crazy.

To this day, I do not know what happened. I have not been back to California since, and my husband and I are going on eight years of marriage and have three daughters.

Living Ghost

Submitted by Melissa

My best friend Darlene and I were about thirteen years old at the time. She lived downtown, on the second story of an apartment building with her mom.

After playing indoors one day, we decided to go outside. As soon as we stepped outside, Darlene in front of me, I said, "It's *so* cold!" and we went back inside to grab my coat off the couch, leaving the door slightly ajar.

Darlene ran back outside, while I stopped at the doorway to finish putting on my coat. I glimpsed her heading to the end of the balcony, where the stairs led to an empty parking lot. Trying to be clever and "scare" her, I began tiptoeing up behind her as she leaned forward, looking over the balcony railing.

When I got about three feet away from her, Darlene turned around quickly, smiled at me, and darted around the corner down the stairs. I laughed and chased after her, only I got an odd feeling—she was nowhere to be found. How'd she get down the stairs and then also find a place to hide so quickly? (Again, the stairs led to an empty parking lot.)

Confused, I circled back up to the balcony and went to the stairs on the opposite end of the lot. This second set of stairs was the only other way between the second floor and the ground level, and was an entire apartment-complex length down. As I made my way down, across, up, and back to her apartment without seeing her, I opened her apartment door, and out walked Darlene. Immediately I thought to myself, *Wtf, how?!*

I said, "How did you get back inside so fast?"

She replied, "What do you mean? I went in right behind you to get my coat, too."

Darlene went on to explain that she had agreed when I said it was cold and went back in with me to grab her coat from her bedroom.

I made her swear on everything sacred to her at the moment, and even periodically until this day (besties over twenty years!), that it was *not* her leaning over the balcony atop the stairs. She continues to promise up and down that she had never even stepped outside.

Did It Want Me?

Submitted by Amanda

To set the scene, I grew up in the boonies of Michigan where the only roads were dirt surrounded by woods. To get anywhere, you essentially drove through a bunch of uninhabited state land.

It was January 2003 around 7:00 p.m. My dad was driving me to my friend's house, about seven miles away. As I mentioned, the only way to get anywhere is by driving all back roads.

About halfway to my friend's house, we saw a pile of coats neatly piled on top of each other in the middle of the road. My dad stopped the car, not thinking much of it. He would frequently hunt those woods and had spent plenty of evenings by himself in them. I'm assuming this is why he was so casual about hopping willy-nilly out of the car.

The moment my dad stepped out of the car, I felt every single hair rise on my body. I felt an overwhelming sense of dread as if my intuition was *screaming* that something was *very* wrong. I started yelling and begging my dad to please come back, to leave the coats and just go.

Every second felt like a minute, and I had the feeling of *something* watching me. My heart was racing, I was shaking, and I started crying from panic. My dad grabbed the coats and tossed them into the back seat while trying to get me to calm down. But the moment he got back into the car and his door closed shut, I heard my father scream at the top of his lungs at the same time I did. I will never forget what I saw.

Outside my window was a man—but not just a normal man. This man was skin and bones. His skin was sickly pale and his hair was long, stringy, and pure white. His arms stretched out like he was struggling to reach me. His fingers were way longer than anyone's should be, with long, jagged, dirty fingernails. His face was sunken in and twisted in what I could only describe as pain or anger. His eyes were a luminescent blue that almost appeared to be glowing. (If you've watched *Game of Thrones*, this man looked like a white walker.) As he stared at me, he began to scream too.

My dad slammed the gas pedal down and sped off as I continued shaking and crying, begging him to tell me that he'd seen what I had. He hesitated at first, but then admitted we'd seen the same thing.

He still dropped me off at my friend's house, even though I didn't want to go anymore. I begged and cried, asking him not to go back home and reminding him that something was not right with what we'd seen. My dad—being my dad—went back anyway, even though he told me he wouldn't.

The strangest part of this experience is that when my dad returned, there were marks in the snow where this *being* had been when he stood outside my car window. There were imprints in the snow of someone standing and sliding backward, as if they had been physically pushed back. There wasn't a slope to the road, and the prints were a solid mark, so slipping on a slope was not an explanation. After the footprints slid back, they showed evidence of something having walked away for about fifty feet, disappearing, and then starting again twenty feet or so later.

I like to think that I had some type of guardian angel (or whatever a protective spirit would be) with me that forced that creature back when it attempted to get to me. This explains why *that thing* was screaming and appeared to be in pain.

My dad doesn't like to talk about what we saw to this day, and I know it terrified him as much as it terrified me.

I've had many experiences on those roads after that, but this was the one that terrified me the most.

I talked to my dad today to find out what he did with those coats, and he confirmed that he did throw them away.

He also told me that the coats were full of pictures of people with their cars. Apparently my dad had gone house to house all around the area with the photos, asking people if they recognized anyone in them. No one did.

My dad also confirmed that this creature had, in fact, looked like a white walker. It felt very validating to have this conversation so many years later.

The Demon That Followed Me Home

My grandparents bought a home in the '60s in an extremely rural area. They moved into the existing home, which is referred to as "the old house" by my family, while they built a new home on the property. This old home is still standing (though in poor condition), across a field and a large creek from the home they built and still live in.

I was twelve years old and riding a go-cart in the field between the two houses. After I made a few laps, I noticed a girl with long, straight, dark hair standing in the window on the top floor of the old house. She was wearing a white nightgown, or maybe an old shift. Nobody had lived in the house for years, and it was getting dangerous to walk up the stairs to the second floor. I thought, *Oh it's just my imagination*, so I continued my lap around the field. When I got to where I could see the old house again, the girl was still standing there. I couldn't make out her face, but I could feel her staring at me. I instantly broke out in goosebumps. I drove back up to the house, and by this time she was gone.

I ended up not going back to my grandparents' house for a number of years due to something unrelated, but the next time I went I was nineteen years old. I drove there to show a friend the old house because I had told them the above story and wanted them to see how creepy it was. This time, I crossed the creek and we got out of my Jeep to look at the outside of the old house.

A few nights later, I had a very vivid dream. In the first part of this dream, I was at a carnival riding the Ferris wheel with a friend. All of a sudden, I felt the stare of the girl coming from behind our seat, while we were in the air. I immediately closed my eyes and covered them with my hands. I felt blood from my friend splatter all over my face, hands, and body.

In this dream, the next thing I knew, I was inside the bathroom in the home where my grandparents actually lived (across the field from the old house). I was in the bathroom and got out of the shower. I turned around to close the shower curtain and suddenly felt the presence of the girl behind me. In my dream, I thought to myself that if I saw her face, I would die. No idea why that thought popped into my head. So I covered my face with my hands again. I felt her trying to pry my fingers away from my face so I would have to look at her.

I woke up screaming at this point and made my boyfriend come to my apartment in the middle of the night to stay with me because I was afraid.

After this, all kinds of strange things began to happen. I would wake up to my dog barking at the corner of my bedroom with all the hair on her back standing up. I started to have nightmares frequently, always about the old house. I would wake up to kitchen cabinets being wide open, but I lived alone and knew it wasn't something I had done.

One night, I went into my kitchen to microwave some pizza rolls. I stood in front of the microwave the whole time. It beeped and the light inside the microwave went off, as normal. And then, in the reflection on the door, I saw feet hanging at the level of my shoulders, poking out from under that white nightgown. I screamed, and all my cabinets flew open. I closed my eyes and covered my face with my hands, terrified that this was the time I would see her face. Then I woke up. It was the most realistic dream I have ever had. I would have sworn it was reality.

At this point, I have decided the girl was an evil spirit at least, or a demon at worst. I knew that when I had crossed the creek a few days before, she had attached herself to me and followed me home.

I continued to have nightmares about the girl for a couple of years, and then one day I had had enough. I knew something bad was going to happen if she didn't leave, but I knew she wasn't going to go willingly, so one night I closed my eyes and mentally pushed her out with all my strength. I told her she wasn't welcome, that she had to leave, that I commanded her to leave in the name of God. I then felt her go. She was gone.

I haven't dreamed about her since. My dog has stopped barking at the corners of rooms. All the other strange things have stopped happening. I truly believe the girl was a demon and that she wanted to kill me. I have never gone back across the creek. I don't let my kids or my husband go across that creek. There is something evil over at the old house still. I feel it.

Forty-Minute Drive

SUBMITTED BY LIZZIE

About six months ago, I was very pregnant with my son and driving home with my daughter after picking her up from her sitter.

Mind you, this was a forty-minute drive, and it was late at night due to construction traffic. Anyway, as I was getting closer to my exit to get off the highway, I went from being very alert and awake to feeling like everything had slowed down, and I was super tired. I remember fighting to keep my eyes open so I would not wreck at seventy miles per hour with my kiddo in the back seat.

I remember the exit sign reading 182 just before closing my eyes. When this happened, I vividly saw a speeding car darting past me to my left and a merging semi to my right. Suddenly, the speeding car lost control, hitting my car and slamming me into the side of the semi entering the highway.

I snapped back awake, saw the exit sign 180, and the same speeding car flew by me—the one I had just seen lose control and crash into me. I waited, making sure it was safe, and pulled over just before exit 182.

As my car stopped, I tried to catch my breath. And then that same car that I recognized flew by me, lost control, and barely missed the merging semi. It slammed into the wall instead. I sat there, shocked. I composed myself and drove home, wondering what had happened.

The Crawl Space

Submitted by Katie

This happened back in 1994 when I was twelve years old. My mom had just married my stepdad, Jim. Jim and his son Vince were visiting us for the summer.

One day it was very stormy. It rained all day, so Vince and I played board games and cards, and otherwise tried to keep ourselves occupied. Later that night, we were sitting in the dark reading stories from the *Scary Stories to Tell in the Dark* books.

Jim yelled up to the room where we were sitting, saying, "Hey, kids, tornado just touched down." He told us to go down to the crawl space in the basement until it passed.

Vince and I grabbed our blankets and books and ran down the stairs. We had never been in this crawl space before. It looked like an old canning room. It was under the kitchen, it had wooden shelves on the walls, and there were even some glass jars left.

We plopped down and continued reading stories, with our parents joining in. The tornado passed by about four or five houses away (and it was pretty bad—some roofs blown off and other damage). Our parents made us stay down there while they checked everything out.

Vince and I, being the nosy kids that we were, started looking around with flashlights and candles. We found a box with clothing in it, which was sitting on an old wheelchair.

My mom and Jim gave us the all-clear, so we went back upstairs with our flashlights and settled into bed. Because of the tornado, the power was out. I am one of those people who sleeps with a fan on, so I knew I was going to have a hard time going to sleep.

Vince was telling me stories about where he lived with his mom when we both heard it: someone calling my name. We jumped up and ran downstairs, finding our parents asleep on the couch. It was late— 2:00 a.m. So we just said, "Oh, it's somebody outside after the tornado."

The next day came, and Vince and I were eating cereal at the table. Suddenly, we heard a loud squeak. My mom came in to bring us some yogurt, saying, "Eat this so it doesn't go bad—and stop that squeaking noise." I told her it wasn't us.

The squeaking noise came and went for a week. My mom and Vince's dad couldn't figure out where it was coming from. One time it would sound like it was in the kitchen, next in the living room, and then the dining room. Then it sounded like it was coming from the office.

Two weeks later, I was lying in bed with cramps and a bad attitude. I heard a voice say, "Katie, come down here."

Figuring it was my mom, I rolled out of bed, put on my pajama pants, and walked down to the bottom stair.

"What!" I yelled, irritated that I had to get up.

Vince and my stepdad turned their heads to look at me and said, "What?" back.

I went on: "Where is my mom? She just called me."

Jim looked at me and answered, "Your mom's been at work. She's not getting off for two more hours."

Then, me with my bad attitude started arguing with them, saying, "Well somebody just called my name and told me to come downstairs."

My mom showed up two hours later, and asked, "Who is the girl in the office?" As I struggled to answer, she continued, saying, "Katie, you're not supposed to have friends over this late." It was 10:00 p.m.

We all looked at her. We hadn't had any guests. We all went back to the office. The door was closed—it's never closed—and music was playing softly on the radio. As all four of us stood in the office, the stations on the radio started changing, then the squeaking noise started happening again. Then the bathroom light came on. I ran out of the room. My mom shut the bathroom light off, turned the music off, and started to walk out of the room, too. Then she turned back, addressing the empty room, and said, "It's too late for this—it is bedtime."

She walked into the living room, where I had joined Vince and Jim. As soon as my mom entered, a smashing sound began in the kitchen: silverware being thrown, plates exploding, objects falling from shelves. When we walked there to see what was really happening, we heard it there, too: a squeaking sound, and then a gust of air passing us. And in the middle of the kitchen there were three forks in a pitchfork symbol, lying on the floor. The ends, not the prongs, were touching. Plates were broken in the sink.

I yelled, "No! Stop! You will not do this!"

Nothing happened after that. We all slept upstairs in our parents' room.

The next day, my stepdad called the landlord, and she answered right away. She then told Jim that before we'd moved in, a girl named Annie had lived in our house. She was twenty-three years old when she passed, and she was in a wheelchair. Annie was mentally handicapped and had the mind of a ten-year-old. Her room was our back office. She loved music and playing with young kids. Her parents took care of her until she died from a stroke. A few years after that, her parents sold the house to the current landlord. Then we rented it two months later.

Annie continued to haunt the house, playing music—sometimes loud but sometimes quietly—messing with everything. She loved to call me downstairs all the time. The strange thing is that while they lived in the house after her death, Annie's parents never experienced a haunting from their daughter.

My mom and Jim think that when we went down into the basement for the tornado and touched her wheelchair, it released her spirit or woke it up. Vince was too scared to go back to the crawl space, or to the office where Annie had once lived. Annie would show herself every once in a while, too. You would catch a glimpse of her in the office window, staring out. She just wanted to play.

Possessed by Flames

SUBMITTED BY REBECCA

A while ago, I was invited to a kickback, a kind of low-key house party, by my best friend Jen. The person throwing the kickback was her coworker, so I had met this person but didn't really know them. Jen wanted me to cook my famous lemon pepper wings. I would get all the ingredients as long as she drove.

Jen picked me up that night and we headed to the kickback. On the way over, she started warning me about the people we were going to hang out with. She told me that Chris, the person throwing the kickback, had a weird obsession with the Ouija board (and that he had ten cats!).

I was a little creeped out by the Ouija board obsession, but I asked if he had one in the house, and she said not to her knowledge. That was all I needed to hear.

You see, I am a strong believer that the Ouija board brings nothing but bad into someone's house, so, as long as it wasn't in the house, I figured I was okay.

We finally pulled up to the house, and it was a cute little home—I immediately saw all of Chris's ten cats in the window! She sure didn't lie about the cats, they were everywhere.

We sat down in the kitchen and I started to get everything ready so I could cook. Chris was super-sweet and welcoming, especially to let me cook in his home. I got the chicken marinated, soaking it in lemon juice for an hour before seasoning and frying it. To marinate the wings, I put the chicken and lemon juice in this bowl Chris's mom had purchased in China. It was white porcelain and covered with beautiful designs.

We all sat down at the table, and everyone began to talk and have a good time. Chris had lit a candle; it was in this weird holder that honestly creeped me out. We then got on the subject of posses-sions. Chris said that someone he had known used a Ouija board and became possessed by it. Jen and I were sitting next to each other, across from Chris and his friend Rachel.

I got this feeling that I should look over at Jen, and then I saw her: just staring at the candle flame, fixed on it without listening to anything else we were saying. I decided to crack a joke, saying, "WTF are you doing, weirdo?"

She answered, still staring, "You don't see it? The girl getting murdered?"

"Uhhhhh, no!" I said. "All I see is a flame!"

Her voice soft, she continued: "Yeah, in the flame, a girl is get-ting stabbed over and over."

She was saying this in such a serious, yet calm, voice.

I said, "Stop playing," and an angry look crossed her face. She muttered, "Who's playing?"

"Jen, for real this is not funny." I tried to get her attention.

Still with this angry face, she said, "I am not laughing."

Then she started hysterically laughing, and said, in the creepiest voice, "Hahahaha, the bitch is dead, and now her killer is just watch-ing me and telling me to do bad things."

I was just staring at her, when all of a sudden the bowl in the sink lifted up off of the sink and slammed back down. I walked over to it and saw that it was in pieces!

Jen started hysterically crying, saying the crazy man in the candle was telling her to unalive herself—and then she got up and grabbed a knife!

After jumping up to stop her, I eventually got her to calm down. I blew out the candle and told her to snap out of it. Then I asked Chris where he'd gotten the weird candleholder. And it turned out, the friend of his who was possessed by the Ouija board had given it to him!

I finally got Jen to snap out of it. She seemed to have no knowledge of what she had just been saying, asking me what had happened. I turned to Chris and demanded, "Where is this Ouija board?" He then admitted that he'd tried burning it, but it wouldn't catch fire, so he'd put it in his attic! So I realized I was in fact in a house with a Ouija board—and not just that, a Ouija board that someone was possessed by . . . and they couldn't burn it?! And guess where the possessed person was currently hanging out? *In Chris's kitchen—it was Rachel!* I said, *"Oh, hell no,"* got my stuff and my best friend, and we left! I drove her car to my house, praying the entire time.

Later on, I found out that on the night prior to the possession, Jen had had a dream about that same man in the flame. Had she had a premonition that she was about to be possessed?

The Stairs to the Attic

SUBMITTED BY TINA

First, a little backstory. Between the ages of nine and twelve, I lived on a farm with my parents, brother, and two stepsisters. The house we lived in was basically four stories tall. It consisted of the attic, the basement, and two main floors. The owners of the farm lived on the first main floor, and my family and I lived on the second main floor.

In the attic was a trunk. In the trunk was a picture of the woman who had supposedly owned the house previously. Every time I went by the trunk, I got the shivers, my hair stood on end, and I felt cold. I hated going into the attic, especially by myself.

The stairs to the attic were a semi-spiral staircase with a sharp turn in the middle. One day, my mom asked me to go up and get some canning jars for her. I didn't want to, but I did it because my mom asked me to. Guess where the canning jars were located? You got it—right next to the trunk! I went upstairs as fast as I could, grabbing as many jars as I could so I wouldn't have to make an extra trip.

I started to go back down the stairs and felt something or someone trip me. As I began to fall, I felt a giant hand on my chest push me upright so I would not fall down the stairs. I went downstairs and told my mom as politely as I could that I would never go back up there to get canning jars for her again—she would have to do it herself.

A while after that, my stepsisters and I got brave and decided that we were going to sleep in the attic overnight. The layout of the attic was an open space with dormers big enough for people to sleep. Next to the big dormer was an old spring bed and a thin mattress. We had a sheet hanging over the opening to the dormer next to the bed, for privacy.

My sisters and I went to bed at around nine o'clock that night. At about midnight, we heard someone coming up the stairs. The steps started at the bottom of the stairs and sounded as if someone walked up about two or three steps, back down one or two, and continued in this strange pattern until they hit the middle of the stairs, when the noises stopped. Then they started again, this time at the top of the stairs. Same pattern once again. Then it started in the middle of the stairs. This went on for about fifteen minutes, after which we heard footsteps start around the attic itself. Then we saw the shadow! My sisters and I fought over who was going to look to see who was there, and we finally decided we were all going to look at the same time.

Whoever or whatever it was walked over to the bed and sat on the edge of the bed. We know this because we all looked out and could see the imprint of their butt on the bed. We watched as it lowered and raised, and we thought that was the end of it.

This happened again about an hour later, only whatever it was never made it up all the way into the attic. It just stayed on the stairs, and then finally left.

The next morning, Mom and Dad talked to us girls about playing on the stairs while we were supposed to be sleeping. What's really strange is that the night before, my younger sister had a dream about a black cat changing into that woman from the trunk and then back into a black cat again.

I was so glad when we finally moved out of that house. I wonder if whatever it was—ghost, woman, cat—is still there, and if the trunk is still in the attic!

Lady in the Window

SUBMITTED BY A.Y.

When I was twelve, my dad, his girlfriend at the time (we will call her Karen, LOL), her eleven-year-old son, her six-year-old daughter, and I were set to move into a large house that had been split into a duplex. This house was originally built in the late 1800s and had likely not been renovated since the 1970s. It had a long driveway leading up to a circle right out front of the building, where we could park in front of the house. We were going to be moving to the second-floor "apartment." The front door led to a foyer which, at that time, had the main door to the left, with our door leading up the stairs to the right. Each of the doors to the duplexes would lock automatically when closed.

As my dad and I pulled up to the house on our first day there, I saw a woman standing in the window on the second floor looking down at us. A cold chill slid down my spine as she smiled and waved down at me. I smiled back at her, although I felt the strangest sense of dread coming over me. I figured it had to be nerves, since this move would be such a big change for me right after my parents' divorce. I thought that the woman I saw had to be the new girl-friend's mom, helping with the move. She did seem to be wearing an old-fashioned buttoned-up pale yellow dress, and her hair was tied up on her head in a beehive style.

I asked my dad if he had met Karen's mom yet, and if she was nice. He said she was, and she was looking forward to meeting me.

I still had a nagging, sick feeling in the pit of my stomach as I explored the rest of the house. When I opened the first door on the right of the stairs, it opened into a narrow butler's pantry with a circular window set high on the wall. It felt like someone had just been in there only a moment before, and I recognized the window as the one the lady would have been looking out of. I was expecting Karen's mother to be really tall at this point.

I looked around the house for Karen's mother and I didn't see her anywhere, so I asked my dad if he had seen her. He said that she wasn't there, and that she wouldn't be until that night, when Karen and her kids would be coming with the moving truck. I was a bit freaked out by this, but I tried to brush it off. I had always been sensitive to spirits as a child, and I was trying to trick myself into believing that I was just upset and nervous and hadn't really seen anyone.

Fast-forward to the first night that Karen's daughter and I spent in our room together. She was sleeping peacefully on her side of the room, and I was restlessly tossing in my new bed. Out of the corner of my eye I saw the closet door open slightly wider. I shut my eyes tight and told myself to stay calm. When I opened them again, I could see by the light of the TV that there was a black hand curled around the edge of the door, and it was inching open, wider and wider. I buried myself under the covers and prayed that it would go away. Everything in my body was telling me to run out the door, but the bedroom door was right beside the closet and I was too scared. I stayed awake under my blanket for a long time before I was too exhausted to keep my eyes open.

The next day I told Karen what I had seen, as I trusted her at this point and thought we were becoming close. But she told me that I was dreaming and I needed to stop watching horror movies and reading so much *Twilight*.

Fast-forward to my thirteenth birthday party. I had some of my girlfriends over to celebrate. We were watching a movie in the living room when my friend Shay and I clearly heard a little girl laughing in the hallway. Karen's daughter was at her dad's house for the weekend, so we definitely thought that was creepy. Later that night, all the girls were sleeping in my room except my friend Shay and me. We were watching TV on a pallet in my room when we heard the laughing again right outside the door. I got up and yanked the door open and we heard the laugh coming from the butler's closet, which was right next to my room. We did not sleep well that night, and after that I always went over to her house to spend the night.

Another night I was walking down the hallway to the kitchen when I heard scratching at the bottom of the steps. The hall light bulb was out, so I just had my phone's light to see by on this side of the long hallway. I was scared, but I decided to keep walking. The scratching stopped and I heard a soft *thump, thump* on the stairs. I turned on the stairway light, and there was nothing there. My dad and his girlfriend were out picking up dinner and her kids were with their dad, so I knew no one was in the apartment. Just when I lost my nerve and started to go back to my room, there was what sounded like someone pounding up the steps on their hands and feet. I cried my eyes out to my best friend about how I knew no one would believe me. I was terrified. I ate dinner alone in my room that night, too afraid to go back past the stairs.

There are more little things that happened, but the one that haunts me to this day was the following incident.

I came home from school and I was home alone. I had started to sleep in Karen's son's room when he was out, because it was the only room I hadn't felt creeped out in since we moved there. I decided to take a nap in there on this afternoon.

As I was sleeping, I started to dream that a black silhouette was standing over me. I could see myself from above, and the figure was leaning in closer. It started to trail its long, black fingers up and down my back slowly. I woke up immediately when I realized that I could physically feel the fingers trailing up and down my side and my back softly, and feel cold breath on the back of my neck. I screamed at the top of my lungs and ran out of the house as fast as I could. I forgot my phone and my house key, so the door locked itself behind me. The neighbors were not home, so I sat outside chilled to the bone for hours, waiting for my dad.

Karen's son said that he would be going to live with his dad for a while because he too had been feeling someone next to him in the bed while he slept. My dad, of course, thought I was exaggerating for attention, and Karen thought I was lying about what had happened to me that day. She thought her son was playing along with me because he just wanted an excuse to live with his dad.

After this, my best friend, who had introduced me to protection magic and the craft in general, taught me a little spell that I could do to help protect me from whatever was targeting me in that house. I started to feel a sense of peace.

Right before we moved out, Karen got a little taste of the things I had experienced in the house. One night, she got up to get something to drink in the middle of the night. She always kept the stove light on in the kitchen, and it cast a light over the very end of the hallway going into the living room. She said that she saw a little girl walk from the living room into the kitchen. She called out her daughter's name and asked her why she was up, and got no answer. Karen walked down the long hallway and into the kitchen when she said she heard a giggle come from the laundry room. When she opened the door, she was surprised that her child wasn't in there. She came and checked our room to find us both sleeping in our beds. She was so scared that we broke the lease and moved out the next week. She never apologized to me, but I'm glad she knew that I wasn't lying!

SPIRIT ENERGIES, BAD AND GOOD

I Escaped Death Twice

SUBMITTED BY ANONYMOUS

When I was younger, maybe twelve or thirteen, a bad tornado destroyed part of the neighboring state. My friend Jackie and her church were going to go clean it up. I am not Christian but decided to go anyway because I wanted to help.

The night before the trip, Jackie, her cousin, and I went to the nearby dam. We had drunk a little bit (I was a heathen back then), but it was only maybe one or two wine coolers, so none of us were drunk. We were walking back to her house and down this smaller road in between two car dealerships. I vividly remember this next part. A semi had come speeding into the road, but it took a sharp turn, and in one moment I was shoving both of them out of the way just in time for the semi to jackknife. I remember seeing the cab coming straight at me but being unable to move. I yelled at Jackie to tell my mom I'm sorry and then felt as though I was falling. The best way I can describe the feeling is like in a dream when you fall and it wakes you up. Suddenly I was standing in between the cab and the trailer—just standing where the cab had ended up. My jacket, which I had dropped at my feet, was now under the driver's-side tire. I later asked my friends if they had seen me move or something, and both did not even remember me almost being hit, but they do remember me pushing them out of the way. They could not recall where I was standing when I did that.

The following day, we got up at 4:00 a.m. and went to their church. We loaded up and drove about four hours to the area where we would be cleaning up. It started pouring down rain as soon as we arrived, but we decided to work anyway with the understanding that we would have to stay away from certain areas due to the weather. We were split into groups and given an area to work on. Some of us were assigned to clean up the park, some were sent to the river beside the park, and others went to the residential area. I was assigned to the residential area.

Right away, I split off from the group. I heard a dog whining and was concerned that it was trapped somewhere. I located the house where I heard the dog whimpering, and it was completely destroyed. While there were parts of the walls leaning onto the roof and other rubble, the entire structure seemed ready to come down at any time. Frantically, I started moving things to rescue the dog and found a tunnel in the debris, where I finally found it. The dog was really a puppy: it didn't look hurt, but it was terrified, cowering in the very back of the tunnel. I turned to see if anyone could help me get to the puppy, as I couldn't risk moving anything else out of concern that it would crush it, but no one was around. And no matter what I tried, I couldn't bait it out—it was just too scared. Ultimately I decided to just crawl in and try to get the puppy out.

I crawled in on my hands and knees and was able to reach it, only getting a few scratches on my back, knees, and arms from the rubble. I lay on my back and basically put the puppy on my stomach and then pushed it so it would be in front of me. I tried to turn around to crawl back out, but I didn't have enough room to do so in that area. So I army-crawled backward, kind of pushing the puppy with my feet until I found a spot where I could turn around.

I managed to turn around just in time to see the puppy take off out of the tunnel. It started barking at me from just outside of it. I remember thinking that it was trying to tell me to hurry up. I tried to do that, but I accidentally kicked what I think was a stud and heard what sounded like thunder. Dust and debris started falling on me, and I knew. I knew that I had somehow escaped death once, and so it was coming back for me that day.

I heard another friend of mine screaming my name, and then I was unable to move again and felt that falling feeling. The next thing I knew, I was standing outside the tunnel unharmed—even the scratches I'd gotten from crawling in the tunnel were gone—with the puppy beside me watching the tunnel collapse. The friend was running full speed at me and just stopped, frozen, and looked at me with a shocked expression on his face. He came over to me and just kept asking me *how?*

He had seen me clearing rubble and was walking in my direction when he saw me bend down. He quickly realized I was in the rubble and started walking more quickly toward me, but when he saw it start to collapse, he called out to me and began running.

Nothing like these two events has ever happened to me since, but every time I wake up from that falling feeling I always remember those times I almost died. I have never been able to explain any of it; never been able to understand or find a logical reason for it. All I know is something or someone didn't want me to die yet.

And before you start wondering, I kept the puppy. His name is Max and he is a Great Dane.

I spoke with Jackie's cousin later, and she confessed that she had seen me in the moments before she thought I was going to get hit by the semi-truck—and had closed her eyes. When she opened them, I was standing in a different place. She thought she'd just been scared, and she didn't realize how close I actually came to being killed.

The guy friend who saw the tunnel incident said he heard a voice he didn't recognize calling out and so he turned his head, and when he looked back he saw me outside the tunnel.

I don't know what made them both look away at the exact right time, and always wondered what they would have seen if they hadn't.

Haunted House

SUBMITTED BY SONIA

First, some backstory. I have always been sensitive to spirits and energies, bad or good. This happened back in the winter of 2013, January or February. We were living in an old house that was built in the late 1800s. We moved there during the summer of 2010. In the years before this event, many strange things had happened, but always small things like my keys disappearing, then reappearing later in odd places like my sock drawer or in the dryer. Also, mostly when I was trying to sleep, I would often hear the sound of slamming doors, and hear voices like two people fighting or arguing. Once I even texted my boyfriend, "Can you please turn down the sound of the TV? I really need to sleep," to which he replied, "I'm outside with Phil [our friend] sitting by the fireplace."

At the time, my son was three and a half years old and my daughter was two and a half. Often when they were asleep, I would hear footsteps upstairs, like kids were running up there. At first, I thought one of them was awake; but when I would go upstairs to check, they were always sound asleep. After some time, I didn't even bother to go look—I just knew.

We had two cats who also sensed these strange happenings. The older was the sweetest big black cat. His name was Charbon, which means "coal" in French. Every single day, Charbon would sleep just beside my kids' door from the moment I put them to bed until I went to sleep. Then he would get up and come sleep in the bed with us as if he were guarding their door, waiting for me to come up to go to bed. That was every single night for the entire time that we lived there.

One time, my kids were with their dad at his parents' house because I needed to study for an exam. I was sitting on the couch studying, and my cats were playing and chasing each other. Their chase brought them into the living room. Buzz, the younger cat, was running very fast, with Charbon behind him, and he suddenly stopped right in front of me in the middle of the living room as if he were coming to a wall. He then raised his head as if looking at someone who was standing there, before going back to his brother to play. I was frozen, wondering what had just happened.

Those are just a few examples of the kind of things that usually happened in that house. Now on to the particular night I want to tell you about.

We were all sleeping. It must have been around midnight or so when my daughter, Jessie, woke up screaming. You need to know that before we moved into this house, she never used to have nightmares, night terrors, or anything like that. So I went to check on her, wondering what was going on, and found that she was crying so hard that I couldn't understand what she was saying. I took her downstairs so my son could go back to sleep.

Downstairs, I kept her in my arms and was trying to comfort her, but she was very upset and continued crying and screaming. After a few minutes, her dad came downstairs to see what was going on, so I asked him to hold her while I got her a glass of milk. I was never able to do that, because as soon as I turned away, she started screaming like her life depended on it. At the same time, she started slapping her thighs repeatedly while looking in front of her as if there were someone standing there, crying and shouting "Remove them!" She seemed physically sick, like something was touching her. She screamed even louder, "Make them go away, Mommy—please!" I didn't know what to do. I was in shock, knowing that something was scaring her to death.

Her dad decided to go to his parents' house with her, as this had been going on for more than thirty minutes and she was visibly terrified and would not go back to sleep. Once they left, I went back upstairs and my son, of course, was fully awake. I asked him, "Are you okay? Would you like to sleep in Mommy's bed tonight?" and we went to sleep in my bed. As I kissed him goodnight and turned off the light on the nightstand, he told me, "He doesn't scare me!"

In my head I was like *WTF?!* I turned the light back on and asked him, "What do you mean?"

He said, "The man there" while pointing at the corner of the room at the foot of the bed. He continued, "Look, he's there. He is smiling!"

And that was enough for me that night! I said, "Come with me, James, we're not sleeping here tonight!" Five minutes later, we were in my car going to my in-laws' house so we could sleep there. I kid you not: I am shaking right now just remembering that feeling.

The day after that, I told my boyfriend "We're moving," and we did. I can live with knowing the house is haunted, but don't scare my kids! Well, don't scare my daughter, at least. My son was fine with it, apparently!

Astral Projection Grandma

Submitted by Rayna

I've had a lot of weird astral projection experiences, but this one happened recently and was absolutely *wild*.

My grandma unfortunately passed away in November 2022. Since then, I have seen her in some positive dreams, which is always a beautiful experience. However, I've also had encounters during astral projection with entities pretending to be dead relatives, and this incident was bone-chilling.

I had fallen asleep on my couch watching TV, when I suddenly felt like I had woken up. I could see my living room, but my surroundings looked fuzzy. This is how I usually know I'm astral-projecting. I looked to my right, where I saw my grandma, along with my mom, looking at me from the corner of the living room. I couldn't see them clearly, but I heard my mom say, "Please come give your grandma a hug. She misses you." I got up from the couch and started approaching them. As I got closer and could see them more clearly, I noticed that my grandma looked different. Her eyes looked dark, her face withered and sad, and I felt this heavy energy surrounding her. I wouldn't say that it felt like "evil" energy: it felt more like deep sadness and loneliness. This was not like my grandma at all: she was always joyful and smiling and cracking jokes, even in her final days. I realized that this entity was not my grandma, but I was overwhelmed by the intense loneliness and sadness that I felt coming from her. I decided to hug her anyway, hoping, whoever this entity was, that my hug would give some sort of healing energy. But as I hugged her, I whispered in her ear, "I know you are not my grandma, but I want to hug you anyway, because I know you need it."

That's when things took a turn.

The woman started crying, wailing, and screaming at me, "I *am* your grandma! How dare you say I am not your grandma!" I pulled away from the hug at that point, but she grabbed on to my arms and shook me violently while continuing to wail, sob, and scream at me. Suddenly, a bright white light flashed around us. She stopped yelling and started looking around, startled by the flashing white light. The entity acting as my "mom" was also startled by the light, and both of them looked around in fear. Suddenly, I was back in my body on the couch, no longer projecting and now physically awake, and they were gone. But my LED strip lights that are plugged in at the same corner of the living room where I saw them *were flashing white light.* This had never happened before. I didn't even have these lights on the white setting—they had been on the blue setting! I grabbed the remote, trying to turn the lights off, but it didn't work. I had to unplug the lights to make it stop. When I plugged them in again, the lights no longer worked!

I told my friend what had happened, and he freaked out and said, "That is some poltergeist shit." This is the first time I've had an astral-projection experience where I felt like it affected something in the physical realm. I was shocked to "wake up" from the projection to the lights flashing, and even more freaked out that the remote did nothing, and that the lights never came on again after plugging them back in.

Alien or Bad Dream?

SUBMITTED BY TAWNYA

When I was about four years old, I shared a room with my brother, who was six and had proven himself to be a deep sleeper. I remember waking up one night. My body felt warm and tingly, almost like I was peeing myself. My heart started racing and I tried to scream for my mom. This was in the '80s, so we didn't have anything like the kid monitoring systems people have today. I was truly panicking, as I couldn't move my body or talk.

I noticed a greenish-colored smoke or fog hovering in a straight layer across the room. There was clear air below it, and it was about five inches above my face as I lay in bed. I lay there paralyzed. I could feel someone or something in the room. And it seemed that as soon as I realized something was there, I also realized I could see a group of little three-foot-tall humanoid creatures—or possible aliens. Whatever they were there for, they were finishing up and immediately disappeared into the green hovering fog.

Then the room started to clear. I sat up and screamed, "*Mom! Mom! Mom!*" She ran into the room and told me it was just a nightmare, got me some water, and ordered me to go back to sleep. I was so scared, it led to a fear of aliens for most of my childhood.

Flash-forward sixteen years: I was twenty then and had just moved in with my best friend's parents, across the street from my childhood home. I was renting the basement but spent most of my time with her family, as I had known them my whole life.

One night we were sitting outside on the porch and my Other Mother, as I call her, started telling a story. She said that late one night, she and her boyfriend at the time were getting home after a concert. Instead of immediately going inside, they continued to hang outside the house. She said they noticed what appeared to be a UFO, high above my childhood home. She described a greenish glowing light or fog. I shouted out, "WTF?! When did you see this? How old was I?" She said, "I don't know, maybe four or five." I just about shit myself.

Do you think my memory is real and aliens were fucking with me, or was it just a bad dream?

The House That Didn't Exist

Submitted by Pernille

I want to tell you about a house that doesn't exist.

Back in 2015, I lived with my boyfriend. We had a good time with our neighbors, who often told us about when they helped clean up abandoned houses after deaths, and often took many good things home and gave the rest to families who didn't have much.

So one day they told us they were on their way to another cleanup at a house that was about a twenty-minute drive away. It had been abandoned for a long time and there were many good things in it. They asked if we wanted to go out there with them.

She said that the house was very old and the front door had become completely stuck so that it was impossible to open. To get in, they had to crawl through a window on the other side of the building. A neighbor told our friends that she had taken out the window and broken it in the process, so the house could be accessed that way.

We decided to go out there with the neighbors. When we drove by the place, we couldn't see the house; just trees and bushes. We found a way around the house through the overgrowth. You could see that it had once been a very beautiful home.

Sure enough, the door was unmovable, and we went around to the other side of the house where the neighbor had said she had taken out a window. However, the window was intact. We guessed that someone must have been there and fixed it.

We took the window out again, and again it broke. We climbed in and looked around the house. It seemed as if the person who had lived there had gotten up one morning, made their bed, and never returned: everything was remarkably orderly, considering it had been abandoned and overgrown for what seemed like years.

I was taken by the bookshelf, where there were many educational books. The first ones were from 1850 and they went right up to 1997. They were all from different fields of study, such as zoology, nursing, and military history. Looking at the bookplates, I could see that all the books had had the same owner, however.

We walked around a bit and tried to get a sense of the person who had lived here, but it was impossible to say how old they had been. Judging by what was left in the place, the owner could have been a four-year-old girl or a hundred-year-old man. Everything was in that house: jewelry, toys from several generations, clothes for all ages and genders; but there was only one bed in the house and only dishes in the kitchen for one or very few people. There was also no evidence of electricity in the house—no outlets, no appliances that would have used electricity—which was quite strange.

We collected a few things, climbed out the window, and drove home.

A few days later, we drove out to the house again, wanting to look around some more. We had almost the same exact experience: the window was intact again, as if it had never been broken; and when we took it out, it broke like the last time. The bed was made, and the house looked as if we had never been in it—everything was in its place. And we hadn't exactly cleaned up after ourselves the other time we were there: there should have been some disorder, books pulled off the shelves, our footsteps in the dust on the floor.

The third time we visited the house, it was a windless day. The window was intact like the other times, and, once again, it broke when we took it out of the wall. When we were done inside the house, I decided to try to open the door from the inside, even though our neighbor had said it was completely stuck. It opened as if it were a brand-new door. Wind started blowing inside the house, and I thought it must be because of the broken window.

My friends left through the door and got into the car with all the things we had found. I was the last one to leave the house, and when I picked up the last box from the floor I heard someone screaming inside the house. It was not a cry from a human, but a scream of warning.

I rushed out the door and ran to the car. When I looked back at the house, the door was closed and the other three asked where I had come from. They said they had come out of the window as we used to do. I told them I had gone out the door, but they didn't believe me. They said the door couldn't be opened. I told them that they had just left through the door, too. They looked at me like I was crazy.

We drove home and shared what we had found among us. Among other things, I got a really nice glass vase that I had not seen before.

We never went out to the house again, as I was terrified after what had happened.

When I drove by the place three months later, there was no house! No trees, bushes, or anything to indicate that there had been a house there, either. I asked my boyfriend about it, but he had no memory of our ever being there or that it had even existed. I tried to find the house on Google Earth to show him pictures of it, but it was nowhere to be found! I could only find the fields I saw when I drove by the place. I tried to go back through my GPS to find the address we had driven to, but the address was not in the GPS, as if our trips had never happened. I then went over to our neighbors and talked to them about it, since they were the ones who had told us about it to begin with. They didn't remember knowing about such a house and thought I must have been stressed and perhaps that it had been a dream. I showed them the vase that I still had at home, but they insisted they had never heard of or seen such a house, and there had been fields in that area for as long as they could remember.

After some time, both our neighbors and ourselves began to dream strange things like our windows being smashed and men walking around our houses at night. We moved out of our house soon after that, and so did the neighbors, and the dreams and sounds stopped. We then lost contact. I met them again in 2019 and talked to them about the house, but they still couldn't remember anything about it. I decided I didn't want to confront them about it anymore.

To this day, I still have the vase from the house that never existed.

Possessed by Myself

SUBMITTED BY CHRISSY M.

I'd just like to start by making sure everyone knows that I'm a fucking moron. I'm not being mean to myself: believe it or not, it's just pretty important to my story.

I guess this is where I put in a little backstory for context. I was raised pretty religious, but now I'm more spiritual than religious. I've always believed in weird paranormal shit—ghosts and aliens and the matrix and stuff.

During the summer I was fourteen, I basically lived at my best friend Brook's house. We were the cliché mid-80s boy-crazy hormonal teen girls, and we spent endless nights pining over the guys on the high school sports teams and pop culture heartthrobs. Brook's older sister, Lanette, was dating a guy on the baseball team, and that gave us an excuse to gawk at all the nice older-guy butts. She was actually pretty cool and let us hang out with her a lot.

I'm really only twenty-seven (wink), but I'm old enough that my first phone was rotary. Brook's family had one of the fancy ones with buttons on it that her dad mounted on the wall. We stretched every inch of the perpetually tangled cord down their hall so that we could prank-call cute boys, chicken out, giggle, and then hang up.

It should come as no surprise that Lanette introduced us to a Ouija board during one of our perpetual sleepovers. She was three years older, so everything she did was cool, and so of course we went along like fucking morons. I told you, I'm a moron. The first couple of times that we played with it, we just asked silly questions about boys, and I'm sure Lanette was the one giving us all the right answers. But toward the end of summer break, shit got real quick. Lanette told us what a Ouija board was really used for—communicating with spirits—and of course we wanted to try. We waited until their parents were asleep, then snuck down the hall to Lanette's room because it was farthest from their parents' room. Lanette had lit some candles for atmosphere, and we sat on her bed around the board.

This happened in the '80s, so I don't remember word for word, but it went something like this. We took turns asking questions. Lanette started.

"Are we alone?" The planchette spelled out "No."

Brook went next. "Are you a boy or girl?"

"You."

My turn. "So you're a girl?"

"You."

Lanette: "Are you dead or alive?"

"Both."

Brook: "Did you used to live here?"

"No."

Me: "Where are you from?"

"Elsewhere."

Lanette: "How old are you?"

"Infinite."

Brook: "Are you stuck here?"

"No."

Me: "What do you want?"

"You."

Lanette: "No. You can't have her. What else do you want?"

"Form."

Brook: "What kind?"

"My form."

Me: "What is your form?"

"Yours."

Whatever we contacted seemed to be picking on me. At least Brook and I were officially scared and told Lanette that we were done. She closed out the session by telling it to leave, moving the planchette to "goodbye," then flipping it over. We didn't play again for a few days, until the last sleepover of the summer. I know I keep bringing it up, but we were fucking morons, because that night marked the beginning of close to forty years of everything from weird or spooky stuff to shit so bad that five different shrinks have failed to help with my own personal little living hell.

We got over the scare from our previous session and decided to try again. As I remember it, we didn't get a response for a few minutes and were about to call it quits. Lanette said something like, "If we don't get contact now, we're stopping," and asked again if any spirits were present. We got a *yes* from the board and, like the morons we were, we giggled nervously but excitedly.

Like I said, this was the '80s, so I'm paraphrasing and I might be wrong about who asked what, but here goes:

"Are there any spirits here?"

"Yes."

"Are you the same one from a few nights ago?"

"Yes."

"What's your name?"

"Chrissy."

We kind of freaked out at that point because that's my nickname, short for Christine.

I remember Lanette asking, "That's our friend's name. You have the same name?"

"I am her."

Brook got a little upset and told Lanette to knock it off. Lanette said it wasn't her and even took her hands off the planchette for a couple of questions.

"You said you want a form. But you can't have hers, so what kind of form do you need?"

"Any."

"Any form? You'd take a boy form? Eww."

"Any."

Then Brook ruined my entire fucking life.

"You can have my stupid Cabbage Patch doll. It's in my closet."

Lanette yelled at Brook and immediately closed the session and put the board away. I don't know what she did with it, but I never saw it again. Not like it mattered: the damage was done. We eventually went to sleep, and my mom came to get me the next day. When we got home, Mom took my Jansport backpack to the laundry room because it had two days of clothes in it. After lunch, she went to do some laundry. She came and found me in my room on the phone with Brook. She had Brook's fucking doll. She asked if I'd brought it home by accident. I said no, we never played with dolls anymore. She said she'd drop it off later when she went shopping, and took it downstairs.

I asked Brook if she'd put the doll in my backpack as a joke, and she swore she hadn't. I told her to ask Lanette, and she ruined my hearing by just screaming down the hall at Lanette. I heard Lanette say "No, idiot!" through the phone. Brook asked if I was sure the doll was hers, not mine, because when we were like nine our moms got us matching dolls. But my mom had made different color outfits so we'd know which one was whose, so I knew it wasn't my doll.

That was the beginning of that fucking doll following me around. We don't have time to go over every instance where that damn thing would show up after I stuffed it in a box or shoved it in the garage or even threw it away. The only time I actually saw it move was the last time it ever made a surprise appearance (I'll get there), but that demon doll would just show up in the weirdest places. I'd put it in the garage, it'd show up on my bed. I'd throw it away, it'd be in my closet. That fucking stowaway even followed me to college, about two hundred miles away. I know for a fact that I put that blue-shirted bitch in a box and left it with my parents before they drove me to my first dorm, but while unpacking on day two, my new room-mate made some comment about the cute doll on the couch. Sure enough, it was Brook's Cabbage Patch pile of shit.

During college, shrink number one tried telling me that I was unconsciously holding on to the doll because of some forgotten childhood trauma. That theory didn't hold any water, because a couple times I'd had my mom and dad put that damn doll away for me and not tell me where it was, only to have that little brunette bitch make her way back to my room or closet.

In my mid-teens it was terrifying. Every time I'd find her, she'd be looking at me. Every fucking time. I'd open my bedroom door and she'd be sitting on my bed facing the door. I'd wake up and she'd be propped up on my homework desk, staring at me. By the time I hit college, she was still freaky, but she had also started to piss me off.

About halfway through the last year of my master's is the last time I ever had to deal with my creepy demon doll stalker. But only because things got worse. My roommate at the time was a bathroom hog, so I mounted a long mirror on the inside of my closet door that I'd use to get ready. If I opened the door all the way and turned my desk chair, I essentially had a vanity. One Friday, I took a short nap after my last class. As I always do, I made the bed when I got up to get ready for a date. I took a quick shower and turned my chair to use the mirror on my closet door. When I opened the door all the way, it reflected my bed. That fucking doll was sitting up against my pillow, watching me. I'd made the bed only about fifteen minutes earlier. I know that bitch hadn't been there then. She definitely startled me. After that initial freakout, I decided to go full fucking moron. I angrily looked at the doll in the mirror and said, "You know, you don't have to stay in that damn doll."

Worst mistake of my life. That's when I watched the doll slump over and fall to one side. Then a dent showed up in the covers like someone was pushing down with a fist or foot. Then another, offset and closer to me. Then another. I was petrified. Something I couldn't see was walking on the bed toward me. Apparently the thing that Brook had given permission to live in the doll took my statement as an invitation to upgrade its residence. I felt something crawl its way up my legs and had that feeling like when someone sits in your lap. Then the worst part: I literally felt my consciousness being shoved out of the way inside my head. I really don't know how to describe it. I felt like I was being stuffed into a box too small to fit me, but only inside my head. It was absolutely shit-yourself terrifying.

The next thing I remember is staring at myself in the mirror. It was the weirdest, most awkward sensation I've ever had. I knew it was me. I knew I was looking at me. But it was like I didn't recognize myself. My right hand moved, but I hadn't moved my hand. My face contorted into a sinister grin, but I hadn't smiled. "Sinister" might not be the right word . . . more like victorious. My body wasn't mine to control. I was watching my body move through my eyes, but I wasn't the one moving my body. I felt my consciousness being shoved aside even more, and my internal self screamed in protest. Next thing I remember is standing in front of my closet and my consciousness being forced back into place. I was seriously freaked out and canceled my date, citing lady problems. I threw on some comfy sweats and threw the damn doll away in the dumpster outside my dorm building. I never saw it again.

Since that first night, I've had hundreds of times when I could feel myself being pushed aside and I'd "wake up" somewhere else a few minutes later. It's never been more than about five minutes and I've never moved farther than I can walk in that time. I've "woken up" with self-inflicted wounds (never life-threatening) and have even institutionalized myself twice.

I mentioned that I've been to see multiple shrinks who haven't been able to help. I've been diagnosed with multiple personality disorder, been told I occasionally enter a fugue state, and even had one guy tell me I'm doing it for attention. I've been to priests, shamans, wisemen, mediums, gurus, monks. The two priests from different denominations gave me pretty much the same response. They essentially said that because the "demon" has the same name as me, they refused to even attempt an exorcism because they might banish my own soul from my body instead of the demon. Thanks, religion.

The best answers that I've found in about thirty years of active searching came only a couple of years ago. I was on Reddit looking for help, and someone claiming to be a seventy-three-year-old woman with "a unique connection" offered to meet. She lived in my city, so I felt more comfortable with a meeting. At my insistence, we met at a popular restaurant where I knew there'd be lots of people. I got there early so I could watch her. I may be moron enough to play with a Ouija board, but as a single woman I'm not stupid about online safety. She really looked to be in her seventies, but I was still a little nervous. After about an hour-long conversation, I felt good about her and we went to her home—her sanctum, as she called it. It was like the physical manifestation of a good "chemical" trip. Given her age and overall demeanor, I suspect she had taken full advantage of the '60s and '70s, if you know what I mean.

She burned some kind of incense and did something like hypnosis to put my consciousness to sleep so she could explore inside my head. Paraphrasing again, but here's what she told me:

The entity sharing my body is female, but isn't a demon. She's a version of me from another plane. Not a past-life kind of thing. I guess most people would say "alternate universe" or something. This version of me died in an accident but found me those nights I fucked around with a Ouija board. She doesn't want to harm or kill me—because if I die, she loses her form again. The times I had "woken up" with self-inflicted wounds were experiments testing the limits of her control. She may not want to hurt me, but she does have a twisted sociopathic sense of humor. I can't have normal relationships, because, without fail, every single time I start to get close to someone, "myself" will take over a few times and ruin it with some fucked-up shit that freaks people out and scares them away.

I call her "myself," because whatever she is claims to have my name. In my mind, there's a distinction between two separate beings.

The words "me, I, my, mine" refer to the real me, while "myself" is strictly reserved for her. I never use the word "myself" out loud, and every time I write or think it, I make the distinction in my mind. So I guess the happy ending is that, in a way no one else will ever fully understand, after forty years of living hell and literal internal struggle, I've come to live with myself.

My First Ghost

SUBMITTED BY ANONYMOUS

This happened in May 2021. I had just moved into an apartment with my brother. I tend to hang on my walls and mirror any picture, loved one's obituary, or award that I have. Although I cannot see myself in the mirror if I'm in my bed, I can see the wall behind my bed and the TV.

Three weeks into living in that apartment, I began to hear creaking noises coming from the floor. At the time, I thought maybe it was just the house settling, because I had just put a large dresser onto the floor in my bedroom a week prior. But I wasn't sure—it sounded like walking. I looked into my mirror, and then I saw it: a skinny figure in the corner of my room. I turned and expected to face it, but nothing was there. So I thought to myself, *Maybe I'm just seeing stuff because I'm not used to being alone.* I come from a big family, so it was a new experience for me.

About two days after that, one of the obituaries fell off the mirror. I stood on my chair to retape it, and through the mirror I saw the figure again. This time when I turned around I could also see it in real life! I looked down at the obituary, then back up, and I noticed that the figure looked just like my friend who had passed away a month before I moved in to the apartment. I smiled at him and cried, because I knew he was coming to say goodbye. After that encounter, I never saw him again.

Mirror Person

SUBMITTED BY ERIC

When I was about eighteen years old, I stayed with this girl I knew, Amanda, for a few months. There were a bunch of our friends that would always come over and hang out during that time.

Amanda would always talk about this man who lived in her mirror. She described him as tall, and he wore like an old-style tall hat. She also would tell us about how she would always wake up with bruises.

One weekend, a group of our friends were over, and Amanda started telling all of us about this man in her mirror again. She then started showing us these bruises all over her body.

I should preface this part by saying that I usually stayed in the bedroom upstairs and Amanda's bedroom was downstairs. So after she showed us all her bruises, I decided to go into her bedroom to look at this mirror. At first I was kind of skeptical, but I really liked this girl and didn't want to think she was lying.

I went into her room and, after a minute or two, I saw it.

In the mirror, there was this dark, almost shadow-like figure of a man in a tall hat standing in the back of the bedroom. I spun around frantically, freaking out instinctively, thinking someone was in the room behind me, but I didn't see anyone.

I looked back at the mirror and the figure was still there.

I looked behind me again. Nothing. No one. But there he was in the mirror.

I'm not sure what came over me next, but it was like something snapped inside me. All of a sudden I just started yelling at the figure inside the mirror, telling him that he wasn't welcome in this house, and that from now on if he wanted to touch her again he was going to have to go through me.

Everyone heard me yelling and came running in from the other room. I started telling them all what had happened, but the figure was no longer there.

I told Amanda that I wasn't going to let anything happen to her, and that I wanted to stay with her in her room that night. I slept on the floor between her bed and the mirror.

The next morning, I woke up extremely sore. I didn't think much of it at first. I just figured it was probably from sleeping on the floor. As Amanda and I joined the others who had stayed the night out in the living room, we realized that I had bruises all over my body. As freaked-out as I was, I had a sense of calm about me, as Amanda felt fine and had no new bruises that morning.

As we were all talking out in the living room about what had transpired, we heard a loud crash. We all rushed into Amanda's bedroom to find her mirror lying shattered in the middle of the floor where I had slept that night.

I still to this day don't really have a logical explanation for anything that happened that night. But as far as I know, Amanda has never woken up with any more bruises.

Premonition

Submitted by Tana

When I was younger, I would have dreams that were more like predictions, or I would randomly daydream of things that were going to happen. Because of this, I was a very anxious child.

Quick background. I am from a small town, and the next town over was only ten miles away, so many people from my town would travel to the next town over for work or shopping. There are many roads that lead to the next town, but the three main ones were Interstate 76, Highway 34, and a county road. My mom would normally take the main road, Highway 34.

One night in the fall, I had a dream that my mom was driving down the county road to get to work. As she was driving, out of nowhere something crossed the road, making her jerk the wheel and roll her car into the cornfields near us. No one could find her, due to the unharvested corn. I could see my mom strapped in the seat, not waking up. I could feel the whole accident, the stiffening of her muscles, the bumps, and hear the glass shatter around me.

I woke up frantic and sore, and I rushed to my mom's room hoping she hadn't left for work yet. Luckily, I had woken up around the time she was getting ready to leave. I started to tell her that she shouldn't go to work, because something bad was going to happen. I didn't want to say what, because seven-year-old me didn't want to relive it. But I begged her to stay home and to call in sick, or say that I was sick. But she still went to work.

As she was leaving, I told her to keep her phone on her where she could get to it just in case. She gave me this weird look and said, "Okay." I still asked her one last time if she could stay as she was walking out the door, but she just said everything would be fine and not to worry.

Not even twenty minutes later, my aunt, who lived two houses down, came over and told me that my mom had just called her and that she had been in an accident on the county road. She said my mom had called the cops, but they couldn't find her. They kept driving past the location of the accident, and all she could hear were the sirens coming and going because they couldn't see any trace of my mom's car with all of the tall cornfields all around.

My aunt came to the house with my mom on the phone still stuck in the car. She wanted me to tell my aunt what my dream was, and to tell my aunt where I'd seen the accident. I was in shock and couldn't move, but was able to work out the location. My aunt and I got in the car and drove down to flag the cops to the location, and they were able to help my mom. She was fine—just a couple of bumps and cuts.

After we were back at home, my mom sat me down and asked me if the bad thing that was going to happen was her getting into a car accident. I just looked at her and nodded. I then asked her how she knew to call me. She told me she'd had this feeling when she drove off but wasn't sure what, and decided to take a different route this time around instead of her usual one. Once she was on the back road, she heard this voice say, "*watch out*," causing her to jerk the wheel and roll.

Still to this day she doesn't know whose voice she heard, and I can't remember if in my dream I yelled out something to her, but I still feel like maybe the accident happened because of me.

This Was My Home

SUBMITTED BY ANA

When I was three years old, we moved into a new home in Burbank, California. My mom had just gotten the keys to the house when she took me over to see it for the first time. When we walked in, I stayed at the front door. Without moving, I told my mom, "This is my home."

She answered, "Yes, baby, this is your new home," to which I replied, "No, Mommy, this was *my* home before. I remember."

My mom looked confused, because this was the first time she had brought me there, and I had not moved from the doorway. So she asked me more questions.

"Oh, it was?" she asked me. "Do you remember what the rest of the home looks like?"

I told her, "Of course," and proceeded to describe the entire layout of the house.

My mother couldn't believe it and started to giggle. Then she asked me, "Who did you live here with?"

I replied, "With my husband."

My mother then started to laugh. "Oh! Your *husband*, huh?"

"Yes, we got married here," I told her.

Then she asked, "Well, where is your husband now?"

"I don't know," I answered. Then I pointed to the dining room and told her, "He murdered me over there, between the kitchen and the dining room."

My mom got scared and told me to stop playing like that. But I wasn't playing. I still have the memories and must have lived there in a past life.

IT WASN'T
A DREAM

Who Was There with Me?

SUBMITTED BY ANNIKA

When I was younger, I always felt like I could see things that others couldn't, or experience things that others didn't. Nothing like this has happened in about eight years, but to this day these two stories I'm about to tell you give me the chills.

The first story takes place when I was in third grade. I lived in my grandparents' house. My mom, my younger sister, and I occupied one room on one side of the house, and my other two family members stayed on the other side of the house. We lived down a hallway to the right, and to the left it led into the living room. There was a mirror hung up on the wall in the hallway right before the opening to the living room. (This is an important detail to remember for the second story.) I've never liked that mirror. I never looked into it when I walked past it—it honestly just gave me really weird vibes.

One night when I was about nine years old, I had just gotten out of the shower. The bathroom was right across from our room, and I went inside and got ready to lie in bed. My sister and mom were already asleep. We always slept with an old VHS playing on the TV since I was afraid of the dark; when the movie was done playing, the screen would turn blue. I remember falling asleep in the middle of the bed with my mom on my right side and my sister on my left.

All of a sudden, I woke up feeling like I was alone in the bed. I felt like the bed had grown in size, because no matter how far I stretched I couldn't feel my sister or mom. Something told me to look toward the door, because maybe they had just gone outside. Then I saw my mom standing in the corner of the room. She was wearing something different than what she wore to bed: she had fallen asleep in shorts and a shirt, but was now wearing a white nightgown. I looked at the TV, which was a blank blue screen, then back at my mother. I could barely see her face, but I remember her pointing to an old camera she was holding and I smiled like I felt she wanted me to. As soon as I smiled, she just walked out of the room— no words were exchanged. I thought nothing of it, because I couldn't explain it. I laid back down and turned to my side, expecting my mom to be gone since she had just left the room, but she was right there! My mom had been sleeping there in the bed the whole time!

I remember staying up the rest of the night staring at the door, because I was afraid my "mom" would walk back in. The next day when I told my actual mom, she brushed it off, saying I was just having a funny dream.

This next story takes place two years later, when I was in fifth grade. I had this really old LG phone that had horrible service, so my apps never worked. I only had one social media app, which was Instagram. I was still sharing a room with my mother and sister. One night we were getting ready for bed. At that time, I slept on the right side of the bed and my sister in the middle. Nothing happened that night, but in the morning everything changed.

I got ready for school like normal and saw my phone was blowing up with messages on Instagram. I didn't think anything of it and just went to school. When I got into the lunchroom, my friends came up to me and asked me why I would send "something like that" to them. I was more than confused, because multiple people were coming up to me saying the same thing. I finally decided to check my phone—and when I did, I will never forget what I saw.

I had made a group chat of fifty-something people (some random, some family and friends), and sent a video to them at 2:00 in the morning. When I looked at the video, it was me, facing that hallway mirror I told you about earlier. I was smiling with my eyes closed, full-on grinning, and in the video I wasn't holding my phone. Instead, the reflection in the mirror behind the "me" on video revealed the same lady who I had once mistaken for my mom. You could only see half of her face and hair.

I just remember screaming and throwing my phone. I remember begging my friends to help me and saying that wasn't me in the video. I ended up showing a teacher, because she asked what had happened; and I remember her face turning pale, then she called my mom to come pick me up. My mom told me to show her the video when we got home. The weirdest thing was that when I went to show her, I pressed on the link to the video and my whole phone glitched and then turned itself off.

To this day, my mom still hasn't seen the video, nor has that phone turned on again. To this day, my friends from elementary school remember seeing the video, though, so I know I wasn't tripping about what I saw.

I never put two and two together before, but writing these stories back to back—I think this was the same person. I'm even more creeped out now.

The Glitch That Made the Doctor Quit

SUBMITTED BY ANNE

This is the story of how a glitch led to our ER doctor quitting his job and having a huge mental crisis.

This happened almost ten years ago. I was new to a small hospital system at the time. One day I was in the break room when I overheard a couple of nurses asking about an ER doctor I hadn't met yet. We'll call him Dr. X. He had been at the hospital for a long time and had treated more trauma and critical patients than I could count. I had heard his name in passing, but at that time I still hadn't met him—which was odd, given how small that department was. It caught my interest when the nurse in the break room asked how he was doing and if he was going to come back.

I went up to them and said, "I haven't met Dr. X before. Is there a reason why he isn't here anymore? Is he on leave or something?" They both paused and one of them cryptically told me he'd had to take an emergency leave of absence. Not wanting to pry, I said something along the lines of "Oh, I'm sorry to hear that." What the nurse said next took my breath away.

A few days before, Dr. X had been on his break, trying to eat something between seeing patients, when his pager went off. There had been a very serious trauma, and he was needed to try to save this patient. As he was rushing up the stairs, a woman stopped him. She looked at him and asked, "How do I get out?"

In a rush, he quickly gave her directions: go down the stairs and make a left, and so on. Then he turned around and raced back to the ER.

When he got to the patient's room, he could already hear their heartbeat monitor flatlining and the sound of the paddles as the nurses on call tried to resuscitate them. He walked into the room and stopped dead in his tracks: the patient was dead. And, he realized, it was the same woman who had stopped him on the stairs and asked how to get out of the building.

Dr. X was not a religious or spiritual man and had never believed in any sort of afterlife or supernatural events. The experience rocked him to his core and caused a serious mental breakdown. I'm not sure if he ever went back to medicine after that experience. To this day, I think about the patient asking him how to get out. I think about how benign that had originally seemed—and then how heavy the actual meaning of it turned out to be.

Glitch in the Woods

SUBMITTED BY LUCAS

I'm from the Netherlands—I was born and raised in a new province from land that was dried from the Southern Sea, so the land itself has no building history. Something strange happened in the early '90s, when I was about nine or ten years old. I lived in the capital city, but our province and city are very green, with a lot of wooded areas.

I used to go exploring in the woods with a friend from my neighborhood. We did this a lot: the idea was to find places where we could build huts. One day we went a little farther into the woods near the area of our homes than we normally did and stumbled upon something very odd. It was a green wooden house, bungalow-style, with a gabled roof and a little front yard. It had a low fence, and the grassy area within it was filled with children's toys. I can remember a wooden doll's stroller with a white and red checkered pattern.

As I looked up from the garden to the house, I saw a man staring at us through the window of what seemed to be the kitchen. He was holding a knife like he was cutting or slicing something. My friend and I stood there in total fear. The man was dressed in all white and had long brown hair and a beard. He looked at us, and we locked eyes. The man still had the knife in his hand, and with his other hand he pointed his finger at us, waving it like he was making a warning sign. We heard no sound at all coming from the house or from the surrounding area. We got so scared that we ran off in complete fear, back to our houses as fast as we could. We promised each other that we would keep what had happened to ourselves and never go back. After a while, my friend said maybe we'd just had the same dream, but to me it wasn't a dream—it was so real.

After a week I got curious. I couldn't comprehend what had happened or accept that it had been a dream, so I went back on my own. I knew my way around the woods. The area was not that big, as there is a provincial road behind it and another housed area. That wooden house just seemed very illogical to me. Our city doesn't have wooden houses. It was a pioneer city built in the '60s, so the only structures are concrete houses made with bricks and mostly flat roofs. This little structure was so out of place.

I went back to the same spot, and the only thing that was left was one green wooden plank. There were no traces of the little house with the low fenced yard, besides that wooden plank.

What was this experience? A glitch of a parallel universe? A vision? A warning?

My Kiddo's Past Life

SUBMITTED BY NICOLE

My youngest son, Bobby, was born in 2010. He was such a good baby—quiet, happy, and sweet; especially when his five years older brother was with him. However, we soon discovered that he had a few sensory issues. His biggest freak-outs involved water. He would fight and cry during bath time if water touched his face. He was also frightened by loud noises such as the vacuum cleaner. We chalked all this up to sensory issues and never paid that much attention to his water aversion. We simply adjusted by using a washcloth to clean his hair and face.

As he got older, though, we realized his fear of water was a bigger problem.

When Bobby was two years old, we took him and his then-seven-year-old brother to a local water park. While my husband and older son went on some attractions, I went to the beach pool with my little guy. The pool started out super shallow and gradually deepened, so I decided to enter the pool in the shallow end and carry him toward the deep end. But the instant my feet touched the water—which was literally less than an inch deep—my kiddo freaked out and tried to climb me like a tree. He was crying and crawling over my shoulder, and I had to immediately turn back and reassure him that I wouldn't try taking him into the pool again. I ended up just playing with him in some little toddler fountains because he wanted nothing to do with standing water.

When Bobby was three years old, we moved to South Carolina. One weekend, we took a trip to Charleston and decided to take a cruise in the harbor to see the fort there and try to spot some dolphins, as well as to tour the aircraft carrier museum, the USS *Yorktown.*

We stood in a long line on the boardwalk, waiting for the ferry tour. As the line moved forward, we evidently stepped out over the water (which I wasn't aware of), but *instantly* my little guy began freaking out and trying to pull me back toward the street. Somehow I knew instinctively that his freak-out was about being over the water. Side note: toddler tantrums are sooooo fun when everyone in the vicinity turns to observe your stellar parenting skills.

This also wasn't my finest gentle parenting moment, because I insisted that we go on the cruise, and I hauled/dragged/carried my son onboard as he wailed and thrashed. He eventually settled down, since the ferry was huge and it was a smooth ride, plus we managed to distract him with the dolphins and other sights.

A few months later, we were walking through a neighborhood park and came across a pond with a fountain in the middle of it. I continued to walk past it, not realizing that Bobby wasn't following me. When my husband and I turned around to see where he'd gone, we realized he was standing in place right in front of the pond. My husband walked back to get him, but our son was in some sort of trance.

My husband asked, "What's wrong, little buddy?"

Our son responded, "I drowned."

My husband thought he'd misheard, so he asked, "What?"

Bobby again said, "I drowned," but he then added, "on an air station in Monterey."

Then he seemed to snap out of the trance and walked on like nothing had happened.

We obviously had no idea what to think of this. I didn't even know what an air station was. I googled it and found out that the Navy had air stations. My husband and I were just as puzzled by Bobby's using the word "drowned," because it wasn't a word he'd ever been exposed to as far as we knew. And we were even more puzzled by his using the name "Monterey." It definitely wasn't something in his vocabulary at his age.

With some more researching to rule out any mention of air stations on his favorite show, *Paw Patrol*, I eventually googled "air station Monterey."

And holy crap. There actually is an air station in Monterey, California!

I found out that it had been active during World War II and hosted Navy divers who would swim out off the coast to retrieve unexploded ordinance that they used during torpedo testing exercises. The air station is now the location of the Naval Academy's officer training.

I've been unable to find any more specific records, such as fatalities from drowning, but regardless—how the *heck* did my son know of such a place and also declare that he'd drowned there? Plus, why did he have such a phobia of bodies of water? I most definitely believe he was remembering a past life.

I Almost Lost Them

SUBMITTED BY CATHERINE

We live in New Jersey, where it used to snow a lot. We lived in Vineland at the time and my dad worked in Berlin. It was about a forty- to fifty-minute ride, depending on which route you took.

About ten years ago, my mom was going to pick my dad up from work. I have four siblings, and one of us would regularly ride with my mom to keep her company. My older brother, who was fourteen or fifteen at the time, wanted to ride with her, but she wasn't too comfortable with it since it had just snowed pretty bad. But he was persistent and told her he *needed* to ride with her, so she said okay. We're all very intuitive, so if we tell my mom we have a feeling, she trusts it.

They were about thirty minutes into the ride, about to get on Route 73. My mother saw that the light was turning red, so she tried to slow down, but hit a patch of ice. She and my brother started to panic because the car was not slowing down and she saw that she was headed straight for a school bus traveling in the opposite direction. My mom started to cry and just grabbed my brother's hand.

As they held hands, everything went silent, and they felt the car and themselves pass through the bus instead of hitting it. They said they could see and smell the inside of the bus. My mother pulled over to gather herself but just couldn't understand how she hadn't hit the bus.

To this day, every time she tells this story, she gets goosebumps and says, "I *know* I hit that bus."

I Still Won't Say Its Name

SUBMITTED BY CASS

From a very young age, I could "read the vibe" a little too well. I would know what was going to happen before it ever did. I could read people in ways that made me look crazy. My "imaginary friends" were all too real to everyone around me. And having this connection to the unexplainable didn't satisfy me—in fact, it made me feel like I needed more answers. I needed to know why I could see things that weren't there, why I could feel different energies, and why any time I would dream I'd be left with a message or in a state of complete horror—until the night when my views changed completely.

One night, a couple of my friends decided to make a Ouija board out of some cardboard, using a shot glass as a planchette. We were all excited to "talk" to something, but that feeling wore off quickly when it seemed like nothing was coming through from the spirit world. It didn't take long for us to give up and quit playing. We thought it wasn't working. I know we were wrong!

The experiences I had as a child skyrocketed in intensity after playing with the board. My intuitive senses about other people were stronger. I saw more things and heard more things I couldn't explain. There was something off—I just didn't know what.

As my mom was getting ready to leave her job one night, she kept hearing a faint cry. She called my dad to tell him. Of course he was cautious, but he told her to head home and that we would go look the next morning. She did not listen. She followed the cries and found three abandoned puppies. She loaded them up and brought them home.

We lived in a very small trailer, so we knew keeping these puppies inside long-term just wouldn't work. So my parents made a deal with my sister and me that they could stay inside until they were healthy, at least. We were over the moon! I had them all stay in my room. There was one in particular that just stole my heart: my little Spiker.

One night, I tucked the other two in and grabbed Spike, getting ready to head to bed.

It felt like we hadn't been asleep long when he woke me up, freaking out and clawing at the window above my bed. I shook it off, as I thought maybe he was having a bad dream, maybe about how his previous owner had treated him. I calmed him down and snuggled back into bed. But as I rolled over with my back toward my bedroom door, the feeling of being watched set in. I lay there uneasily with my head covered by the blankets, and slowly I started to hype myself up to turn over and look. Finally, I turned over with my eyes barely open and saw a man standing in my room, wearing a trench coat and a tall hat. He was watching me. I quickly closed my eyes, telling myself to start screaming to wake my parents up. But I couldn't—I was too scared.

After what felt like an eternity, I mustered up the courage to sit up and yell for my dad. As I sat up to yell, I turned to look in the direction of the man I had seen, and my door slowly began to open! I jumped out of bed and ran to my parents' room. I was inconsolable.

I didn't sleep in my room after that for almost four months, and I would not go in there after the sun went down or if the light was off.

Fast-forward a couple of years. We were living in California when I stumbled across a TikTok series about this thing that fit my description of what I saw that night. When I saw it, I instantly started crying because I knew I had experienced what the woman in the video was experiencing! I sat there and watched all the videos she had on her account in complete fear. Remember that Ouija board we made? Well, this thing can attach itself to you through the misuse of a Ouija board or other spiritual device. This thing is resilient. The more you talk about it, the worse the activity you experience. I'm almost twenty-four years old and I still refuse to call it by its name, and it still gives me chills to this day.

The moral of the story is, don't search for things if you're not ready for what searches for you. This thing goes by many different names. I will not be providing them for my own safety and yours. But I'm sure if you look up my description, you'll find what no one wants to find!

Baby Alive

SUBMITTED BY LEAH

One Christmas when I was around eight or nine, my nana got me a first-generation Baby Alive doll. Unlike the ones they make today, it had a fully animatronic head. It moved its mouth when it ate and talked, and it blinked and closed its eyes when it went to sleep. Other than the head, there were no other moving parts on the doll. My nana said it was the only one left in the whole store when she got it. She said she found it hidden behind other things on the shelf. They were the most popular toy that year, so I was very grateful that she got it for me.

The whole day after I opened it, it was the only toy I played with until it was time to go to bed. I put the doll to sleep so its eyes would close, then turned it off so it would "sleep" with me all night. The next morning when I woke up, its eyes were wide open, staring at me. I checked the on/off switch, thinking that maybe I'd flipped it on in my sleep, but it was still off. I thought that maybe I didn't close her eyes and I just imagined that I had.

I played with the doll all day long, until about 5:00 p.m., when I remembered I had a new Operation board game that I wanted to try out. So I tucked my baby into bed, putting her into sleep mode with her eyes closed, her body safely under my blanket up to her shoulders. I then went to start opening my game. I was trying to put the game together when I heard tapping from behind me. I turned around and my baby's arms were straight up in the air, not under the blanket as I had left her. I was very confused, but thought *Maybe I didn't tuck her arms in.* Maybe I had just left them that way by accident. So, once again, I put her arms under the blanket and tucked her back in.

I went back to my game and had just finished putting it together when I heard the tapping again. I turned around and, again, the doll's arms were pointing straight up into the air. This time I knew 100 percent that I had tucked her arms in, but I pretended like everything was normal and just did it again. I decided that maybe my new doll didn't want me to play with my other toys, so I put the toy I was playing with back in its box, and when I turned around again, her head was facing me with her eyes open. I didn't know what to do. I was scared, but at the same time felt like maybe my

Baby Alive was actually alive and I had to protect it. I also wondered if my grandma, who had passed away the year before, had possessed it. Either way, I had to take care of this Baby Alive that could possibly be real—or possessed.

I told my nana about the things that were going on, and of course she didn't believe me. Then I told her I wanted to bring the Baby Alive to my mom's house because I didn't feel safe leaving it alone. The Baby Alive continued to just stare at me randomly when I slept with it even if it was off. Its legs and arms would move to different positions, even after I took the batteries out, and with no mechanics in the legs or arms. Then one day my brother got ahold of it and ate its silicone face off, and my mom threw it away. Goodbye, creepy Baby Alive.

Glitch in the Matrix, Nightmare, or Haunted House?

SUBMITTED BY CHICA

Years ago, when I was still living in New York, I had what I can only describe as the weirdest thing ever happen to me.

Let me start by saying I have always been afraid of our basement. It's an unfinished basement with a dirt floor and massive spiders and crickets everywhere. Our washer and dryer were down there, and unfortunately my mother used to make me do the laundry all the time. So, as you can imagine, I was extremely afraid to go down into the basement to do the laundry. I also could swear that there was something evil lurking in that basement.

On this particular night, I had a dream—or at least I think I did. In this dream, the door to the basement opened on its own. I was extremely afraid, so I tried to run back upstairs where my parents were, but something grabbed me as I got near the top of the steps and started pulling me back down toward the basement. I tried to scream, but I couldn't.

My dad had a chair in the foyer right next to the basement where he would always come home and take his shoes off. As I was being pulled toward the basement, I grabbed on to the chair, and as I did, his shoes got caught on the legs and moved also. I ended up letting go, which left both the chair and shoes in the middle of the foyer close to the basement door. I started praying frantically, and just like that I awoke in a cold sweat. I did not go back to sleep. At daylight, I slowly made my way downstairs; to my horror, the chair and shoes were exactly where I had let them go in my nightmare, and the basement door was open. We never ever leave it open!

I asked my dad and mom if they had moved the chair and shoes. They both said no. To this day, I cannot explain this.

Marsh Road

SUBMITTED BY REBECCA

One day my coworker and I were talking about scary stories. We were sharing experiences, and one she told me creeped me out!

We are going to call my coworker Cara and her girlfriend Sara. Cara and Sara and some friends went out one night. One of the friends—we will call him John—was obsessed with ghost-hunting. So when he said, "Let's go up to Marsh Road in Milpitas," everyone assumed it had something to do with his primary interest. The group asked him what the significance of Marsh Road was, so he told them this story.

A sixteen-year-old boy murdered his fourteen-year-old girlfriend. He was going through a rough time and, to make matters worse, she was trying to break it off. He became so angry that he snapped and killed her. He then took fourteen different couples up to view her body. The last couple that saw it felt guilty and went to the authorities. The boy was arrested and is still in prison today. The legend says that whoever goes up to Marsh Road in groups of two will have multiple things happen. First, the girl will appear in the rearview mirror—but whatever you do, *do not slam on the brakes.* If you slam on the brakes, the girl will reappear in your back seat. Second, a red truck will appear out of nowhere and chase you off the road. Once you are off the road, the truck will be gone—which is weird, seeing as how Marsh is a one-car road in the mountains. There is no place to turn around.

After hearing this story, the group of friends decided to go up to the road. It was weird enough that they were intrigued, and they wanted to see if what John said would really happen. They got to the road and Cara started getting scared. Cara is the type of person who doesn't get scared in situations like these, but she just had this uneasy feeling.

While on the road, John decided to pull the car over to the spot where the girl had been found. He got out of the car, and everyone started getting mad at him. Why had he added another stop to their trip? Then John opened his trunk. And guess what he brought? A Ouija board!

At this point, Cara was pissed. Cara liked ghost-hunting, but she drew the line at the Ouija board. John started to ask it questions, when suddenly the group looked up to see truck lights speeding down the mountain toward them. John threw the Ouija in the trunk—which, as you may know, leaves the portal open for spirits who might pass through—and they sped off. He checked the rearview mirror, and sure enough: there was the girl. The red truck appeared next, chasing them. Once they got to the end of the road, the truck was gone, which is impossible! They would have at least seen the truck reversing, as you cannot turn around on this road.

After this experience, John became obsessed. He wanted to go up to Marsh Road every weekend. And while most of the time his friends ignored him, finally they decided to go up one more time. It was then that Cara had noticed that John was starting to have a short fuse. John also had something going on with his eyes. They would turn black when he was angry. They lost contact shortly after, and she felt something demonic around.

After my coworker told me this story, I decided I had to try it for myself. I love ghost-hunting. I had no idea that this would be the last time I would ever want to go. I decided to go with this guy we called Greeneyez. He was very annoying and kept wanting to scare me, but he also had a car and was willing to drive. We also went with two other people, a brother and sister. We'll call them Lina and Chacho. Chacho was up front with Greeneyez, and Lina was in the back with me. We attempted our trip, but the first night we tried, we got lost.

Instead, we decided to go to the east-side hills in San Jose. There are stories of an albino camp in the hills. It is said that the people in that camp only come out at night. They are not the albinos that we think of, normal people whose skin and hair have no pigment. These albinos, by contrast, are completely deformed.

Our car was driving up the hill when suddenly a rock came flying at us, hitting the side. That was all we needed: we sped away and never looked back! We then went to a nearby park and started to relax, just talking and joking with each other. Then, off in the distance, a weird humanoid creature appeared with an unusually long neck. It wasn't like any animal I have ever seen. In my opinion, it was some sort of demon. I wish I had gotten a picture of it.

I was through with ghost-hunting for the day, feeling uneasy, and we all agreed to go home. But the next day, the entire group wanted to try again. I agreed to go, so around five o'clock we headed back to Marsh Road. We were in the same seating arrangement: Chacho and

Greeneyez in the front, me and Lina in the back. And this time we did not get lost. We headed up to the road, and we reached the place where the girl in my coworker's story had been left for dead. We turned the rearview mirror up, though, because we did not want to see the girl. Suddenly, Greeneyez slammed on the brakes!

I spun around, yelling at him, saying, "I literally told you what happened to my friend, and what they said *not* to do!" Don't hit your brakes, or the girl will get in your back seat.

Greeneyez, irritated by my criticism, took off, going at least fifty miles an hour around very narrow mountain roads. I noticed that a truck was following us, slowly at first, but then it started speeding. When we got to the end of the road, I turned around again, and the truck had disappeared. Then, once we hit the main street, Greeneyez got out of the car and lay on the road! I was cursing him out at this point, asking him what the heck he was doing. Then he said that he had seen the girl, and she had told him to unalive himself.

Chacho looked into the mirror and started counting, "1, 2, 3."

I said, "What do you mean 1, 2, 3?"

"I see three of you back there."

I said, "Yeah, okay."

He turned down the mirror and there she was: the reflection of a translucent teenage girl with short black hair, smiling at me! All of a sudden it started to feel like the right side of my face was on fire, the side closer to where the girl in the mirror's reflection was sitting. I didn't say anything, because I just wanted to get out of the car!

Then Lina said, "Is anyone else's face on fire?"

I said, "What side of your face is on fire?"

IT WASN'T A DREAM

She said her left, which would have been closer to this girl! I still didn't say anything. Lina started crying. I asked what was wrong, and she said the girl was laughing at her. I yelled at Greeneyez to pull the car over—I felt suffocated and uneasy, and I needed air. We finally got to a gas station, and I told my friends what I was feeling.

We got back into the car, and we made it to our house. When the car stopped, we heard the loudest *pop*. We jumped out to see what had happened. My whole car battery was detached from the car! I looked back in the car and saw the girl again, this time in the front seat and smiling at me. I was traumatized by this point.

Incredibly, after all this, my friends still wanted to go to low-rider night (a night where all the lowriders in San Jose come together and cruise). I just wanted to stay home, but I went and nothing weird happened. We got back home and Greeneyez wanted to sleep in my car. I thought this was weird, but I let him. While I was in the house, something told me to look out the window, and I saw Greeneyez in my passenger side and a huge dark shadow above him.

After this incident, I never talked to these people again. They have too many dark spirits around them.

Catwalk

SUBMITTED BY TAWNYA

We grew up in the '80s, so as kids we rode our bikes everywhere until the streetlights came on. Our neighborhood was tight. All the kids hung out all day, we slept at each other's houses, and we were close, like siblings.

One day my older girlfriend Angel and my little cousin decided to go on a bike ride. There was a small shortcut through what was called the Catwalk. It connects the neighborhood to the school and created a shorter walk for the kids who walked to school rather than taking the bus.

When I was little, the older kids talked about the Catwalk leading to the past or the future. As kids, we were all scared of the stories of children getting lost that way and never coming back home.

I was ten years old and bored, so I stupidly allowed Angel to talk us into riding our bikes down the Catwalk. It was getting close to the time we should have been heading home for dinner, and we were by the school, nowhere near home. But of course, like the little followers we were, we rode behind Angel down the Catwalk, pedaling as fast as we could.

As we entered the neighborhood, something felt off. My cousin, who was a few years younger than me, began crying in a panic. We both felt confused and scared. Angel, on the other hand, was in heaven, proud that she had the balls to finally do the Catwalk. My cousin was crying, and I was looking around for someone other than us who might be able to help. But the street was quiet. There were no sounds, no birds, and the wind was calm. It was eerie. We rode up the street and there were no people, no movement—everything seemed to have stopped.

I said to Angel, "Hey, girl, let's head back," and she agreed. We turned to head through the Catwalk going the opposite direction. It was gone—and there were graves in its place.

Angel said, "Wait a minute . . . maybe we rode too far." I could tell she was starting to get scared. We rode around five or six times, but no Catwalk.

After about an hour, we all started crying and trying to figure out how we'd gotten so lost. We sat on the corner for just a second, then looked up—and the Catwalk was right in front of our faces. We quickly got on our bikes and rode as fast as we could through the Catwalk and back home. We didn't look back. We pedaled so fast, not even talking as we pedaled. And when we got home, we assumed we would be in trouble since we had been gone for at least an hour or two. But when we walked in the door, my grandma just told us to get washed up for dinner. No time had passed. We realized we were right on time, as if we had never gotten lost. Glitch in the matrix, time-traveling kids—I don't know. You decide.

THOSE WHO DON'T BELIEVE

Grid in the Sky

One night I was on the back porch stargazing and having a chill night in the dark by myself. I was living at my parents' house and couldn't smoke inside, so I took pleasure in waiting until everyone fell asleep to finally get some alone time. Well, on this specific night, I spent some time staring up in awe at the sky and having my normal epiphanies about life on earth. Everything was fine until my phone died. I got up, walked inside, and plugged it in to charge in my room.

It wasn't until I reached the back sliding glass door and opened it up to go outside again that things started to feel very off. Now at this point I had been smoking for a while, so it wasn't the weed just beginning to kick in—but I started dissociating really badly. It was like I'd stepped out of the "real world" into a virtual reality video game, and nothing felt real. I'm not sure what the explanation was for the shift, but I sat back down anyway to try to shake it off because I didn't want to freak myself out.

A half hour went by, and I started putting my stuff away to go back inside and lie down (it was about 12:30 a.m. at this point). I took one last look up at the stars. I blinked a couple of times and, while doing so, I started to see a full-on grid appear. I squinted my eyes, even looked away and then back again to see if my retinas were just messing me up, but it was real, and it was there. My heart dropped and I shot up out of my chair with my mouth wide open, yelling in my back yard, "Does anyone else see this?!" I completely lost my cool because I couldn't believe what I was witnessing. In the wake of all that, I immediately thought about that scene in *Chicken Little* where he tells everyone the sky is falling but nobody believes him. So after being the neighborhood alarm, I *sprinted* inside to get my phone and hopefully take a picture. I grabbed it off the charger, ran back outside (the grid was still there), and tried powering it on, but it was still completely dead. Thirty minutes of charging and nothing. I looked back up, and the grid had disappeared. I was so mad, because it was one of those moments that I knew that nobody would believe me unless I had feasible proof or evidence, but, through some strange coincidences, I came up with nothing.

Here's what I remember: the grid appeared to have medium-sized interconnecting squares that created a dome-like shape encompassing the sky in bright neon green. It was also fairly close to my view, kind of at the same level a bird flies, with a point in the middle where the lines got slimmer as they reached the top. It looked like a hologram you would see in a movie or something. I definitely feel like I wasn't supposed to experience that, and for a couple of days after it happened, I had intense paranoia. But eventually everything went back to normal, although I still don't know how to wrap my head around what happened.

It's been almost five years since then, and the crazy thing is that it wasn't what I was smoking, and I know that for a fact. I finished the rest of my stash in the following days after that without incident, so I know what I saw wasn't me going into psychosis or greening out. I was a seasoned stoner with an incredibly high tolerance. It's just weird because that shift that I felt when I opened the door disappeared the minute the grid went away. It felt like I was in a spiritual realm of some sort. This is the sole reason why I believe firmly in the simulation theory! I've shared this story with a select number of people, including family members, who immediately invalidated it. It would be nice to find anyone who has any information or has gone through the same thing—that is why I am sharing!

Camping Alone with Vanishing Gnomes

SUBMITTED BY AMY

Last summer I was on a road trip by myself and booked a campsite in Quebec, Canada. I'm not very good at French, and as I pulled up to the campground I realized I had accidentally booked a campsite at their version of Santa's village: a tourist trap set up to be perpetual Christmas-time, hung with twinkling lights and other yuletide decorations. But it was dark when I arrived, so I laughed about it and figured it was no big deal, then set about trying to find the site I had reserved. I was having issues finding the site-number markers, and instead kept finding these little miniature houses with gnomes in front of them. The homes were the size of gingerbread houses, and the gnomes were no bigger than a small plastic water bottle. Eventually I found my site, set up my tent in the dark, and went on a little walk around the area to see the lights. I also sent a message to some friends of mine about how funny the gnomes were. At midnight, I crawled into my tent alone and went to bed.

In the middle of the night, at some point I got up to go to the bathroom, and then turned around and returned to bed. Then, around 4:00 a.m., I was jolted awake again: a black-eyed demon child was wrestling me, sitting on my chest, choking me and trying to kill me. He had what I can only describe as dark, deathly eyes, looked like a demon child, and was 110 percent not human. I wrestled it and tried to fight it off me. I started repeatedly saying, "What the fuck" while fighting. I was able to push it off, and I was awoken into this reality by the sound of my own voice, and the demon melted away. I feel like I woke up a second time. My tent was identical to a few seconds before, my body in the same position, but the demon was gone. At this point I was thinking that it must have been a nightmare, but my chest was tight and I could feel pain on my neck where the demon had been choking me. It also felt like someone had been sitting on top of my chest in the spot the demon had been, and it was tight and sore. I felt like I had crossed into another universe.

I got back to sleep and woke up around 7:30 or 8:00 a.m. I got up and began to pack up my site. I decided to go for a walk first, because I wanted to go take pictures of the gnomes I had told my friends about the night before. The problem was, as I walked around the site, the little gnome houses were still there, but all the gnomes were gone. The night before, I had shined a light on some of them and remembered there being cobwebs around some of the gnomes as if they had been there for a very long time. I was dumbfounded, walking around and seeing the houses with no gnomes all over the campground. The gnomes had been there when I went to bed, I had told my friends about them, they'd had cobwebs on them—but after the demon came, the gnomes had disappeared without a trace.

That morning, I packed up my car and left the campground. The whole experience was incredibly odd. I kept thinking that maybe the gnomes were a game for the kids; but the timeline, cobwebs, and placement wouldn't make sense. The demon also felt so real. I couldn't shake the feeling that I had somehow crossed into an alternate universe for that night, or the demon tried to pull me into one, and scared the gnomes away. I'm a logical person and have never experienced anything like that. I also haven't told a lot of people about this story, because it genuinely sounds ridiculous and make-believe. Now, though, as I look through more videos on TikTok about things like this, I feel so much less crazy.

Verified Ghost

SUBMITTED BY LATOSHIA

This is a story that I always tell those who don't believe. Most of my family have had interactions with those who passed on. I saw and talked to passed loved ones and others when I was younger. But as I've grown up, how I see and interpret spirits has changed and evolved. When I was a teenager, I felt like my "abilities" had faded or been blocked. That is, until I moved to Tennessee with my mom, and all kinds of paranormal activity started happening in our new home.

We had a family friend, my mom's friend Jodie, staying with us while we were going through some difficult family drama. One of the first things that happened was when Jodie said she kept seeing shadows in the sitting room. Then my mom's boyfriend was in the bathroom and suddenly ran out yelling, saying that he had seen a shadow. He said it came toward him and he felt it pass through him, as cold as ice. Shortly after this happened, Jodie and my mom's boyfriend moved out, as they were both freaked out. My mom had a job that kept her away from home for long periods of time, so when they left, she had to quit due to not having childcare any longer.

The next time something weird happened, it happened to me. I was lying in bed listening to the radio when I felt someone staring at me. I looked at the foot of my bed and saw a floating gray woman. She had a gown on and was just watching me. I was so scared, I couldn't move. Finally, I was able to sit up and hit my overhead light switch; when I looked back, she had vanished. It had not been fully dark when I saw her originally, as I'd had a small lamp on, so this was not a trick of the light. I didn't say anything at the time, because I was worried I would just be brushed off or called crazy, as that is what was said about the family friends who had talked about their encounters.

It wasn't too long after that that my verified ghost encounter happened. My mom was home that evening and had been across the yard at the neighbor's. It was dark outside. Before she had visited the neighbors, she had told me to fold the clean laundry, put it away, and put the empty basket in her room so it would be there when she got back. I finished the laundry and went to return the basket to her room. As I entered, I hit the light switch and I saw and heard the Venetian blinds crash against her window. There was a shape of a human at the blinds, which had disappeared as the blinds slammed down. Our blinds were super-heavy and could not be moved without force. Wind could not have moved them—the window was closed and no amount of airflow could have caused them to move so violently.

After I saw the figure disappear and heard the blinds slam down, I dropped the basket and ran to the living room. Minutes later, my mom walked in and yelled at me, saying, "What were you doing staring at me through the window in my room?" I just looked back at her in confusion, almost in tears. She said it had freaked her out and given her the creeps seeing me staring at her walking across the yard. I finally explained to her, in tears, what had happened, and she said maybe the figure everyone had been seeing was my guardian angel. She then told me that she, too, had been seeing a woman recently while she was on the road working, so it was not just happening at the house.

Later on, after we moved out of that house and away from the drama we had been dealing with there, the lady stopped appearing. But we knew we had seen the same thing at the same time from different points of view. This has helped me know I'm not crazy, and it has helped me validate my other experiences.

The Little Girl in the Corner of My Bed

SUBMITTED BY CHERISH

This is a story about my weird (but sweet) experience of a dream that happened approximately four years ago, in early 2019. I can vividly remember it to this day, every detail of it. So here goes.

In my dream, hubby and I were asleep, and I was woken up by someone pulling the blankets in the corner of our bed, touching my feet. "Mommy, Mommy, wakie wakie, it is time to wake up." Still very sleepy, I opened my eyes slowly and looked to where the voice was coming from. Standing in the corner of our bed was a little girl with curly hair down to her shoulders, about three or four years old, wearing a light pink dress. I could not see her face clearly, as it was still dark outside and we only had a little night light on my bedside table.

She was pulling the blanket, asking me to get up. I just casually said something like, "It is still dark outside, darling, go back to sleep." She did not say a single word, but she just stared at me and kind of floated to the dark corner of the room and disappeared. That is when I "really" woke up. I sat up and looked around, and then shook and woke my hubby and asked, "Where did our little girl go?"

He stared at me, confused, and said, "What are you talking about?"

I looked at him and just answered, "Oh." I realized in that moment that we didn't have a child (yet). At the time, we were actually trying to have our first baby. I shrugged it off and thought that it was just a dream, then went back to sleep, but I remember feeling weird—kind of hollow and sad the morning after.

I kept thinking about the little girl in my dream for weeks after that incident. I didn't feel scared of her, but what I felt was this sense of longing. She didn't show up in my dreams again.

Fast-forward to a few months later: we found out that we were pregnant and having a girl. I didn't really think much about it until a couple of nights ago, when that dream happened in real life. Hubby and I were asleep. I was woken up by my daughter in exactly the same way as in my dream four years earlier. There she was: a little girl wearing a light pink dress (she loves dressing up as a princess and wears a dress to bed sometimes). She also has curly hair down to her shoulders and she is now three years old. She said, "Mommy, Mommy, wakie wakie, it is time to wake up," and I noticed it was still dark outside. I looked at the clock: it was 4:00 a.m. I had a strong feeling of déjà vu and realized that this had happened before in my dream. But this time, instead of saying "Go back to sleep" to my daughter, I invited her to come into our bed instead. She snuggled next to me and whispered, "I was watching you, Mommy. I chose you." Then we fell back to sleep.

When I think about that dream now, it could have been me having a glimpse into my future as a mom.

Did I Slip into an Alternate Universe?

SUBMITTED BY SOPHIA

In 2016, my mother got pregnant. I am now seventeen, but to this day I can recall vivid memories of when she was pregnant: going to the ultrasounds, finding out it was a girl, the baby shower. I remember every aspect of it. She had the baby two months after my tenth birthday, on April 27, 2016. I know she had that baby. I have a shirt in my closet that says "Best Big Sister" on it that I got as a birthday present on my tenth birthday from my grandma. I am the youngest child. I have no younger siblings. I remember helping my mother come up with a name, Valerie Jade. I remember her getting a yellow baby stroller at the baby shower, because when we got home, we joked about the ugly and obnoxious color of it. I know she was pregnant.

The day after she had the baby, it disappeared. *Everyone* agreed that she was never pregnant. They told me it had just been a dream. But how do you dream about nine months of your life? I still have the T-shirt that says "Best Big Sister" on it hanging in my closet; but, again, I'm the youngest child. I remember every aspect of her pregnancy, but there's no baby to show for it. My family calls me crazy, but I know she was pregnant. I don't know if this was a glitch or if the universe just has it in for me.

Danny and Jon

SUBMITTED BY AMANDA

I have two stories that I would like to share with you.

For some context, ever since I was a little girl I could pick up on spirit through different psychic senses, although not always the same ones. Sometimes it was smell, other times it was visual or clair-audience. But regardless of the way I was picking up on spirit, I could always telepathically get a message from them if I opened myself up to receive. As I got older, these senses got stronger.

My mother, on the other hand, is a very spiritual person but is not clairvoyant like myself. She often senses an energy shift in the room or feels like she is being watched, but that is about it.

My mother would, however, have intense dreams about spirit visits. In fact, my cousin, who tragically passed very young, would often bring spirits to my mother in her dreams for her to help. My mother often didn't know what to do with these spirits—most of them were children—but she would just talk to them and ask them questions.

On to the first story:

One night, my mother and I were both asleep under the same roof. I felt an energetic shift in my room that woke me abruptly, like a hit of adrenaline. In the past, when I would feel this kind of shift, I would be worried about a spirit attack of some sort. However, once I was wide awake, I could sense that the energy I was experiencing, although intense, was completely harmless. And then I saw it: a little boy around age four, with a white T-shirt and brown cargo pants, was zipping all around my room, doing cartwheels and jumping off all my furniture. It was so fast. I tried to track him with my eyes as he zipped back and forth, but it was almost impossible. My then-fiancé also woke up and asked, "Can you see that?" I was shocked, as he didn't believe, as I did, in spirits, and would often give me crap about connecting with them. But as it turned out, he didn't quite see the same thing as me. Instead of a little child, my fiancé told me that a scary-looking man was staring at him. I followed his gaze to where he was looking and realized I could see him, too. But although he looked rough and "scary," I got spirit guide energy from him, so I didn't worry about his presence. I almost felt he was the child's spiritual babysitter. Eventually the little boy stopped by my bed, made a cheeky face, and then shrank into a ball—and *pop*, he vanished. It was like watching a bubble burst.

I was very interested as to who the boy was, but decided I'd figure it out in the morning and went back to sleep.

In the morning, my mother came out of her room looking very tired. I asked her how she'd slept and she said she'd had a very strange dream. I asked her about it, and she said she dreamed that she was outside of a house with a young couple. She is a real estate agent, so she felt that she was conducting a house viewing. She was standing outside this house for a while, just chitchatting with the couple about what they were looking for. Then she noticed that the area of this house was unfamiliar to her, but that didn't worry her.

While talking, my mom kept getting distracted by a little boy in the front window of the house. He was jumping around, yelling, doing cartwheels and making silly faces. Eventually, after a few minutes of this behavior, my mother asked, "Is that your son? I think he is trying to get your attention." The couple looked at each other with confusion and sadness and said, "That can't be our boy, he died last month in a tragic accident." My mom was so shocked by what they said that she woke from her dream.

Interested to see who this little boy was, I opened myself up to him in hopes that he was still nearby. He was, and the information I got shocked me. He said, "My name is Danny and I am from the sunny coast," which is an abbreviation for the Sunshine Coast in Queensland, Australia.

I asked him if he needed our help.

He said, "I am scared to go home. My parents are mad at me."

I then asked, "Are your parents in spirit, or alive?"

And he answered, "They are alive."

I asked, "Why would they be mad at you? They love you."

He said, "I was very naughty. I played with the lighter and now they have nothing."

He showed me a barbecue-style lighter with a long nozzle and a child-lock slider. The child lock was not engaged.

I asked if he'd passed in a house fire, and he said yes. I told him he needed to be brave and that his parents missed him a lot and that he should go home to see just how much they miss him. He took a minute to just sit with me before he decided to take my advice and leave and head home.

Later that day, I was searching online for articles about a house fire in the Sunshine Coast where a four-year-old boy had died. My jaw dropped when I found *the* article. It spelled out exactly the scenario that Danny had described when I communicated with him: the house burning down with the little boy inside. The barbecue lighter. It was amazing confirmation, but also devastating. I often think of little Danny.

Here is the second story I have for you.

For a lot of my teen years, my main spirit guide, Jon, was very visibly and physically active in my life, especially when I was trying to sleep. It actually got to a point where I had to ask him to not be so present because he was waking me up so often. He was a beautiful male guide. He was African, six feet tall with very dark skin. He liked to lie or sit across the end of my bed, and often would slowly pace around my room. He always brought such calming energy, but he always woke me when he would get on the bed, as it would physically shift.

One night, I woke up with that same burst of adrenaline. I didn't know what was happening, but I was on alert. I looked to the end of my bed, where I saw Jon pacing frantically. He was putting his hands on the top of his head, rubbing his face, and just freaking out. Before I got the chance to ask what was wrong, he ran toward my wall and disappeared. I tried to go back to sleep, but I was concerned by Jon's very out-of-character behavior.

After about five minutes had passed, there was still no Jon. I heard the tap turn on outside my room, and I got up. My mom, with a very flustered expression on her face, was having a drink. I asked her if she was okay, and she said she'd had a horrific dream. She said it was like sleep paralysis. She was sleeping on her bed and woke up to a red-headed girl on top of her. My mother was frozen and couldn't move or even scream. The girl was taunting her with a knife—pretending to stab her and slit her throat, and then laughing. All of a sudden, the girl's face turned to rage, and she swung the knife back, about to stab. My mother said she thought she was going to die. Suddenly her bedroom door burst open and what she described as a tall African man came in, grabbed the girl by the hair, and yanked her off my mom in one swift movement. The girl screamed as she was being dragged away, and my mom made a comment about how weak and small she looked in the man's hands. He shut the door behind him, and mom awoke from her dream.

I was like, "Oh my god, you saw Jon—he came to save you!" All of it made sense to me, and I was so appreciative that Jon had decided to step in that night, even though it wasn't his job to.

I no longer have Jon as a guide, as I outgrew him, but I do miss him dearly.

Something in the Sorority House

SUBMITTED BY KELLY

I went to college in Buffalo, New York. The college housing area is in an older part of the city with some really, really old, creepy houses. My freshman year, I joined a sorority, and my sophomore year I decided to move into the sorority house. The seniors who were grad-uating told all of us that the house was haunted, but we brushed it off and thought nothing of it.

There were six of us who moved into the sorority house that year. The first night we moved in, I heard creaking stairs all night. I really thought someone must have gotten a million midnight snacks. But the stairs were *loud* and keeping me up, so I decided to see who was causing all the ruckus. I stepped outside my room, looked around, and no one was there. I, for some reason, had the courage to make sure all the doors were locked, and they were. I checked the other six rooms. Everyone was fast asleep. I ran to my room, pulled the covers over my head, and didn't move until morning.

I ended up convincing myself that I was just hearing things and tried to forget about it. A couple of days later, one of the girls ran into our room, screaming, "It wrote on the mirror!" Eventually, after catching her breath, our roommate Jen told us she was talking on the phone with a friend while getting ready, when she heard her foundation makeup bottle hit the floor. She turned around and, written on her vanity mirror with her foundation was the word "HI." It was clear as day. Jen was very shaken up by this, but the other girls in the house honestly didn't believe her. I told them I'd heard creaking stairs all night the first night we moved in, and it had to be the ghost the older sorority girls had warned us about. The other roommates still didn't believe us.

We went a few weeks without much ghost activity in the house. But one night, all six of us were in our roommate Melissa's room talking about what we were going to wear to a party that night. We were all standing on the right side of the room by her closet. On the left side of her room, her blow-dryer was plugged in but wasn't turned on. All of a sudden, the blow-dryer turned on full-blast without any of us touching it. We tripped over each other, running out of the room down the hall while screaming bloody murder. The blow-dryer eventually turned itself off after about twenty seconds. The boys next door said it must be electrical and it was all in our heads, but a blow-dryer turning on and off on its own doesn't really seem like the result of a wiring issue to me.

The other roommates finally believed Jen and me that this house was haunted after the blow-dryer incident. While we were talking about the ghost and trying to come up with a game plan, Jen said, "Doesn't this ghost feel like a girl to you guys?" We all agreed and felt like the ghost was a teenager, and we all had a gut feeling about it. Jen said, "Maybe she just wants to be friends and be included?" The midnight snacks, makeup, and blow-dryer (all girly things) made us think she just wanted to be a part of the group.

So, we named her Gwenevere, and called her Gwen for short. When we were all together hanging out, we would make sure to acknowledge her and say, "Hey, Gwen, we are gonna watch TV, do you wanna join us?"

After we started including her, most of the ghost activity stopped. Every now and then we would be in a room hanging out, and, if we forgot to say hi to her, the lights in that room would turn off. We would say, "Hi, Gwen! Sorry we missed you over there." We would have to flick the switch a couple times and it would eventually turn back on. Sometimes the lights would come on in empty rooms. When we used to have parties at the house and take pictures of our night, there would always be tons of orbs in all the photos. We knew Gwen was at the party with us.

Gwen was a friendly and kind ghost. She just wanted to hang out, play practical jokes on us, and be a part of the crew. We got really lucky and were sad to leave her when we graduated. We made sure to tell the younger girls moving in about Gwen and that it was important to always make her feel included.

Did He Want My Baby?

SUBMITTED BY DANIELLE

A few years ago, I started dating my now-husband. His whole family is very spiritual. Before she sadly passed away, his aunt used to communicate with a higher power and spiritual guides. She was very happy about us dating because she said we were very strong together. But she also said we had to be careful, because some of the guides said that not everyone was happy about the fact that our energies had come together—they were just too strong. I didn't understand what she meant when she said that, and I kind of brushed it off. We got married a year later, and all was good; no bad energies or anything.

But I remember I used to get these really weird dreams. Very vivid. I would wake up shaken and sweaty. Once I dreamed that a snake wanted to bite me, and I was trying to escape from it, and a lady passed by me and said, "Just let him bite you. He will leave after." And then I woke up.

Another time, I was taking a nap, and I had a dream that I was in an underground cave. Everything was made of rocks, and it was black and hot. I remember I was sweating and there was fire around me. I was lying down on a flat rock, and my wrists and ankles were restrained with metal chains. Around me were four men in dark-red cloaks, but their faces were covered. Two were standing next to my shoulders and two were standing at my feet. Then came a fifth man. He had a black cloak and his face wasn't covered. He was pale and bald.

I started getting nervous as he got closer to me. He stopped between the two men who were at my feet. I started screaming and asking, "What do you want?!" He pointed to my stomach. He had long, pointy black fingernails. I screamed, "No! You can't have him! I won't let you have him!" His nail was getting closer to my stomach, and I screamed and fought and eventually woke up crying. My husband was holding my shoulders, telling me I was screaming in my sleep and he couldn't wake me. It was terrifying. The next day, after I'd had a chance to calm down and think about what had happened in the dream, I took a pregnancy test: it was positive, and later I gave birth to my first son.

But that's not the creepiest part.

Fast-forward a few years. I had, by that point, given birth to two healthy boys, and we had completely forgotten all about my dreams. Everything was calm.

Then one evening I was watching a TV show called *Paranormal Encounter* (or something like that) where guests talked about their experiences. A woman was introduced and began talking, saying that a few years before, she had been babysitting a little girl. At that time she was pregnant, and the girl's mother told her that if she needed to rest, she could use the bed in their guest room. At one point, the babysitter went to sleep. She said she had a nightmare. But she described *my dream*—from the cave, to the chains, to the five men in cloaks, to the fingernail pointing at her stomach! But in her dream the man scratched her stomach, and sadly she lost her baby.

I was in shock. To this day, I have no idea what I experienced. All I know is that it still terrifies me to think about it.

Russian Nurse

SUBMITTED BY JUSTIN CALDER

I lived in Russia for a couple of years in my very early twenties. One of the cities I lived in was about three hundred miles south of Moscow. My working partner and I lived in a hotel room because the local government didn't allow foreigners to rent apartments. One afternoon on the way back to our hotel, we missed the bus. Rather than wait another hour for the next one, we decided to just walk, because it wouldn't take us the full hour anyway. To cut even more time off our walk, we decided to cut through a large, forested park area.

On the outer edges there were walkways and benches, grassy areas, and a few picnic tables. There was one path that led straight into the trees in the direction we needed to go, so we headed that way. An older lady, maybe in her sixties, called out from a bench, saying something like, "I wouldn't go that way."

To be polite, we stopped and asked, "Why not?"

"It is not as it seems."

"It's more difficult or longer than it looks?"

"No. Ghosts from our past live there. It is not as it seems."

That's actually not as odd a statement as it may sound. Russia is an old country, and its people have very old superstitions and beliefs based on around fifteen hundred years of history. Unpopulated areas are generally considered to be haunted. Not a "scary movie"-type haunting, just that ghosts are real and they hang around places where live people aren't present.

We were both twenty-year-old guys, so we assured her we'd be okay and continued on the path. My partner commented about how the lady smelled like smoke, but not like the typical cheap Russian cigarettes. I'd noticed it, too, but thought nothing of it. Only a few yards into the trees, the concrete path disappeared and became nothing but a rough outline of a dirt trail, which was obviously rarely used. The farther we walked into the trees, the less of the path we saw: it was more like a memory than anything distinct, like time was hard at work brushing away the last remnants of something man had already forgotten.

There wasn't any particular feeling as we walked in the relative quiet of the forested area. We could hear the bustling city outside and the birds and rustling leaves inside. After maybe ten minutes, we both noticed the same smoky smell as had lingered around the old woman. Nothing like we were in any danger of a forest fire, but the smell that haunts an area *after* a large fire. We could see that the trees were thinning ahead, and the dirt once again returned to concrete. We exited the trees and saw a typical Russian building; it looked like it was built of huge concrete Lego blocks with windows evenly spaced in the two levels. We approached at an angle, so we could see all three dimensions. It wasn't huge, two stories high, maybe ten windows long and four wide. A sign on the front told us it was a children's hospital. We could see a couple of kids staring out and watched a nurse or doctor draw the curtains across a window.

The closer we got to the hospital, the stronger the smell of smoke was. Russian hospitals were government property and off-limits to us unless we were patients, so we just kept on the sidewalk outside the small metal fence. We waved at the kids we saw and even got a couple of hesitant return waves. Soon enough, we were past the building and headed back into the trees on the far side of the property. We didn't see a parking lot or any cars, but we figured it must have been on the other side where we couldn't see it as we walked by.

We both noticed the smoky smell dissipate as we got farther away, and eventually it disappeared. We made it through to the far side of the forested park and back to regular city sidewalks. Later that week at an English class we taught, I asked my class about the odd children's hospital in the middle of the park. The entire class went dead silent and just stared at me for a moment. Then someone asked a grammar question and class resumed.

Yuri, one of my older male students, caught me after class before we all left. He asked how I knew about the hospital, and I told him our story of walking through the park to get back to the hotel. He listened as growing confusion showed on his aged face.

When I finished, he came in close and all but whispered, "I wouldn't tell anyone about this. It is forbidden." The Russian word he used is a mix of "forbidden" and "suppressed," like the unspoken concept behind why you keep a secret.

Of course I asked him why. Again, in whispers, he told me that there had indeed once been a children's hospital in the park, but it had burned to the ground in the '70s. There were rumors that ranged from an accident to faulty wiring to a government conspiracy to keep illegal government medical experiments from being discovered. Yuri said the only survivor had been his mother, who was a nurse there. She survived the fire but died suddenly in a different hospital while recovering from smoke inhalation.

I felt the color drain from my face. He noticed and looked at me for a moment.

"You saw her, didn't you? She likes to sit on a bench that used to be at the property line of the hospital. I go visit her sometimes. I can't always see her, and she very rarely speaks to me, but I can always smell the smoke that means she is there."

I Want to Go Down There

SUBMITTED BY GABRIELLE

Back in the summer of 2020, when Covid had just begun and I was still in high school, some friends and I had decided to go to a tunnel that is supposedly haunted. It was a four-mile walk to the tunnel, eight miles round-trip, so we all drove and met each other nearby. It wasn't fully dark when we got there, so we started our walk. It all started out so smoothly: we were walking, making jokes, and even saw a little waterfall (the waterfall is an important key to understanding this story, so we'll come back to it).

It started to get darker, so we picked up the pace a little bit so we could make it to the tunnel at a decent time. It felt like we were talking for so long. We thought we had walked almost two miles or so, because it was already 10:30 and we had arrived at 7:30. We got to this area and it sounded like there was running water, so we assumed there was a stream somewhere near us. My ex-best friend kept saying things like, "I want to go down there" and "I want to see what it is," but I just knew it wasn't a good idea. Leading down to where she wanted to go, it looked like a straight drop, so I wasn't going to allow her or myself to go down.

We finally reached the part of the walk where there is a little bridge, and we walked across it. Five minutes after walking across this bridge, I stopped dead in my tracks because I saw this big, black tall figure. I mean, it looked like it was a nine-foot man standing in front of me, but it was just a shadow. I yelled at everyone to stop moving and asked them if they saw it, too. Most of them said yes, and we started running. We kept running and running for what felt like hours. I finally saw the waterfall, so I told everyone that we were almost back to our cars and could slow down. We started walking again. At that point, the group was kind of split up, but we could still see each other.

My ex-best friend pulled me to the side, and all of a sudden we were back at the area that sounded like it had running water, and she told me, "I want to go down there, please let's go." I just grabbed her hand and told her to run with me. We started running for what felt like ten minutes, and we saw the waterfall again. Those areas aren't that close together; they're maybe a mile away from each other. We kept running and made it back to the cars. Everyone asked what had taken us so long. I still have no idea what happened and why we got pushed back to that strange area, so far away from everyone else.

AS CREEPY AS
IT SOUNDS

Dark Figures

SUBMITTED BY AMANDA

When I was about fifteen, I woke up in the middle of the night to a thick, heavy feeling in my bedroom. I instantly felt my gaze drawn to my full-length mirror, which was behind my bed—so I had to look up to see it as I was lying down. Standing next to my mirror on the right side was a black figure. Mind you, this was the middle of the night, and we lived in the country, so the only light in my room was the moonlight coming through my bedroom window. As a result, it was very dark in the room. This figure was completely black, so much so that it stood out in the darkness of my room. It had short curly hair, almost like a clown wig. But it had no facial features. Solid black. I remember having the distinct feeling that it was female. So I thought, *Mom?* although I was sure it couldn't be her. Being a kid, I threw my covers over my head. We all know that those covers are a magic force field, right?

I must have fallen asleep, because the next thing I knew, I was awake again, and once again felt that heavy feeling in my room. And again, my gaze was drawn to the full-length mirror behind me. On the left side of the mirror, there now stood a different figure, just as black as the one that had stood on the right side earlier that night. The one on the right was not there anymore, but I could still feel its presence. I could sense that this new figure was male. It had a haircut like the kind men had in the 1700s. I don't know how I knew the sex of the figures. It was just this strong feeling that each one seemed to give off. I was terrified!

It was at this moment that I felt the instant intense sensation of needing to throw up. To get out of my room, I had to get past the figure that was standing next to the mirror. I looked back up at the mirror to now see that the other figure was back! So now there were two: the figure to the right and another to the left. I noted that neither figure had a reflection in the mirror. I remember thinking, *How can that be? They are both standing at an angle at which they should be seen in the mirror.* I bolted up because I was gonna puke and there was no stopping it. In terror, I ran past both of the figures, *brushing up against one of them!* I literally felt it *whoosh* through and past me at the same time!

I ran around the corner of my bedroom door to the bathroom. I threw up so hard, it felt like it came from my toes, like my body was purging itself. I sat on the bathroom floor for quite a while, terrified to go back into my bedroom. After some time, I mustered up the courage to go back into my room. I only had to reach around the corner of the bathroom door frame and bedroom door frame to reach the light switch in my room. I was so scared that something was going to grab my hand. The air in my room was thick—I could feel it when my hand entered my room. I switched on the light and looked in the room. Nothing! They were gone! I don't remember what exactly happened after that. I am pretty sure I went back in and slept with my covers over my head and the light on.

To this day (I am forty-six now), that was one of the scariest nights of my life!

The Dream Thief

SUBMITTED BY EMILY

Let me set the scene for you. I was young, between nine and twelve, and lived in Ohio. We had just moved to an old house in the middle of nowhere. To the left of our back yard was a hill, and behind us was a small patch of woods. We had one neighbor, and everything else surrounding us in all directions was fields as far as you could see, which was as creepy as it sounds.

When we moved to this house, my mom, brother, and I all felt a feeling of "wrongness" there. Within the first week of our moving in, I started sleepwalking and began seeing who I call "the dream thief" *every* night for the entire three years we lived in that house.

I've always had very realistic dreams that feel as if I'm awake and I can't tell I'm dreaming. Because of this, the experience I'm about to share felt as real to me as if it were happening in real life.

The third night in the new house, I went to bed and started dreaming. It was a normal dream like always: I was at school walking through the halls with my friends, chatting and laughing. Every time we passed a classroom, I would glance in the door and see my teachers. When we were walking past the math classroom, I looked in the room again and saw a man I didn't recognize. He was wearing dark clothes and just had a darkness about him, like he was covered in a shadow. He was glaring, staring right at me, and I could feel the same sense of "wrongness" that I felt at the new house.

The second I noticed the man, a feeling of fear instantly took over me, goosebumps covered my body, and my friends and surroundings disappeared. Suddenly I was standing in my new bedroom, staring out the window into our back yard. It was night and I could only see what the moonlight shined on. I was unable to move or speak and was stuck at the window filled with a feeling of dread.

Staring at the back yard I noticed the same man that was staring at me earlier start to creep over the hill and sneak across my back yard, clearly not wanting to be noticed. I tried to run and yell for my mom but still couldn't move. The man was getting closer to our house, headed for our back door, and all I could do was watch. I somehow knew he wanted to get inside and that he was there to do something horrible.

Knowing my family was asleep and in danger, I had to make sure this man didn't get into our house. All of a sudden, for a reason unknown to me, I could move again. Immediately, I turned and ran to make sure the back door was locked and we were safe. As I ran down the stairs and through the kitchen, I could see the man at the door right in front of me. I crashed into the door and felt the knob rotate in my hand.

I turned the outside light on and found myself staring into the face of the same man. He looked like a normal person besides the evil glare pointed right at me. Slowly, he reached for the doorknob, while staring into my eyes, and then *bam*—everything went black; it was like I'd passed out.

The next thing I knew, my mom was waking me up. We were outside and I was lying in the grass in our back yard. My mom said that she woke up to all the kitchen lights on and me missing from my bed, but all the doors and windows were shut and locked.

This exact dream, with the same man, happened every night for three years. Every night, I would go to bed and dream a normal dream, then at some point I would notice that man staring at me. In every dream, I would then be suddenly transported to my bedroom window, where the same situation would again play out. Every morning, my mom would find all the kitchen lights on and the doors locked. Some mornings I would wake up in my bed, and some mornings my mom would wake me up in the back yard like the first time this happened. She quickly realized I was sleepwalking but could never figure out why I went outside or how.

After we moved into a new house, I never had this dream again, never again saw the man in a dream, and I never sleepwalked again. To this day, I have no explanation for what happened.

It's Freaking Me Out!

SUBMITTED BY HAYLEY

In 2007, my grandmother passed away. She raised me until I was twelve, when she got sick, so this was absolutely devastating for me. Then, in 2012, my uncle passed away from a sudden heart attack in his sleep. This was also super hard, because we were close. In 2014, my brother passed away on Christmas Eve. Again, super fucking hard—and at that point in my life, I was just so ready to give up. This is all important.

Fast-forward to a couple of months ago. I have always had trouble sleeping, but nothing like the problems I started to have. I would sleep only twenty to forty minutes a night, and I kept dreaming the same thing. I knew I was dreaming, but it didn't feel like a dream: I was walking down a long white hallway with blue doors lining the sides. I distinctly remember feeling like I wasn't supposed to be there. Suddenly, a very odd-looking woman would appear next to me before I got a chance to open any of the doors. She looked like me, but also not like me at the same time. I have blue eyes, she had green. I currently have black hair, she had blonde. My hair is also curly and hers was board-stiff. She also had this super-wide creepy smile. Once she smiled and touched my arm, I would instantly wake up and not be able to go back to sleep.

One night in my dream, I decided that I would open the first door I came to. I opened it and entered my grandparents' house, where I had grown up. Sitting on the couch was my brother. He was the same age as he was when he died, but, as I stood there staring at him with my jaw on the floor, I noticed he looked older, like he should have looked today. He noticed me staring, and he said, "Why are you standing there like an idiot?" At that moment, I started bawling and gave him the biggest hug ever. Suddenly the lady appeared, and I woke up. I still smelled like him and woke up standing in the middle of my bedroom with my arms like they were still hugging him! My face was also wet because I was actually crying. It was insane.

The next night I decided in my dream to go to the door across the hall from my brother's, because now there was a lock on that first door that wasn't there the previous night. I walked through it into my uncle's living room. There, in the chair, wearing nothing but his tighty whities, screaming at the TV, was my uncle. I didn't gawk, because I knew I didn't have time. I just ran over and wrapped my arms around him. He seemed shocked, but still wrapped his arms around me in a tight hug. I told him how much I loved him, and when I opened my eyes the lady was standing there behind him. Same thing again. When I woke up, I could still smell him and my face was wet. The difference was that this time I woke up in my hallway, not my bedroom. It was about the same distance as it would have been between the doors.

The next night, I went to sleep and I was ready. I booked it to the next available door and ran right into the kitchen of my grandparents' house. Standing at the sink was my grandmother. She turned, looked at me with a smile, and said, "Hey, baby! I didn't know you were coming today." She wrapped her arms around me and I completely broke down. In typical fashion for her, my grandma never asked what was wrong, but just held me while telling me it would be okay. I told her repeatedly how much I loved her and how sorry I was that I hadn't turned out like she'd hoped I would. I didn't even have to open my eyes this time. I knew the lady had come for me. This time I woke up farther down my hallway, smelling like my grandma, and I was crying so hard that I was hyperventilating.

After that, I would fall asleep and there was no hallway. I would just go right into a different place—a place where they were all still

174

alive and life was much different. I learned that in that place I am married, have two sons (I have four girls here and wouldn't trade them for the world), and I'd followed in my family's tradition by joining the military (in this world, I am a nurse). Every time the lady would come and I'd wake up, I'd find myself in a different part of my house. This has been going on every night for months. It's never been the same "dream," and it was like days had passed there at the same rate as they do here. I don't know what the hell is going on, but I don't sleepwalk, and they don't feel like dreams to me.

Rewind

Submitted by LaLanya

This happened many years ago when I lived in New Hampshire. My husband (now ex), our two young kids, and I went on a day trip, but it was cut short when it started to rain. We headed home, with me driving. This part is weird, because I never drove when my husband was with me, and I don't know why I was driving on that day. We were having a great time singing and joking around with the kids, enjoying the drive, when suddenly, as we were coming down a steep hill, a car pulled out in front of us. The rain-drenched road kept me from being able to stop, and we barreled into the other car.

The crash was horrific. I was the only one who survived. As I screamed and cried, trying to get to my children, everything stopped.

I was being pulled backward in time. I watched as we reversed out of the wreck and back up to the top of the hill. At the top of the hill, we started moving forward again, but this time there was an arrow on the ground showing me the route to take to miss the car, and how to get back over it again before a large truck topped the hill coming from the other direction. Time, once again, stopped. We reversed backward back up the hill. I felt myself snap back into my body, and we were once again on the top of the hill.

I said out loud, "Holy shit! Hold on." My husband looked at me, confused. I took the route just as it had showed me in my second vision. I just missed both the car that did in fact pull out in front of us, as well as the truck that topped the hill just as we got back into the correct lane. My husband looked at me again and said, "How did you know that car was going to pull out in front of us?" I just said, "I had a vision." Never before or since that day have I had another one.

The Thing under the Trampoline

SUBMITTED BY SHAYLA

I have a large family. Growing up, we had family get-togethers every summer, and we always picked a different relative's house as the location—most often, we met at my aunt or my uncle's place as they both had large properties. The guest list, after all, is pretty huge: I'm talking like twenty-plus kids and teens and then the adults and family friends. We would always have late-night campfires. When they were over, the parents would usually go drink and talk inside, and, being kids at the time, we all would stay outside and play in the dark.

My aunt's home was kind of in a forest-like area, located in the Canadian Shield, which is very rocky and rugged—lots of granite and hills and rivers. She had a trampoline that the kids (really pre-teens at the time) always played on. We particularly liked a game called "popcorn," and another one that was a little dangerous, but always a good time: someone would go under the trampoline and try to poke or grab the passing feet of the people on top. If the person underneath touched you, then you were now the person who went down there.

One night after playing, we all were hanging out lying out on the trampoline, when all of a sudden something under the trampoline started poking us. We were terrified. We all started screaming and the older teens came running, and then we all saw something white run into the forest next to us. It wasn't big, maybe like the size of a large dog. We couldn't make out what it was. An animal? A person? None of us could agree.

The next night, we had another gathering at my aunt's house, where we carried on as usual. But the question of what we had seen came up, and we all decided to go to the trampoline to find out if the thing we had seen would return. We waited and waited and waited. This time the older teens were there with us, hoping to catch a glimpse, too. But after an hour or so, nothing had happened and the thing had not returned, so we started playing our usual trampoline game again. Then, as we were about to send another unlucky person to the space underneath the trampoline, something white came running out from the forest and scrambled underneath it. I don't know how to explain what we saw. It was blurry because it was so fast, and it was a ghostly white. It went under the trampoline and started poking us, like last time—the only difference was that now the older cousins were also seeing and feeling it. It had strength, just like a person. We didn't know what to think. The younger cousins were too scared to look underneath, but the older ones were not. They looked, but the thing ran into the forest so fast again that it was just a white blur.

We ran and told our parents. Of course, they thought we were lying. We told them to go see for themselves, and they did. My mom, my aunts, and a family friend went out. After about twenty minutes or so, they came running in literally screaming. They'd seen it, and it had poked them, too.

Every year, this thing would come out and do this, and it became our new game with whatever this thing was. We were scared of it, but it never hurt us. My aunt ended up getting divorced and moved, but we will never forget this white thing from the forest. Everyone still talks about it to this day, and it's been about seventeen years. We still don't know what it was, and we will never be able to describe it to the point where you could really picture what we saw. We all still think it was pretty creepy that we played with it.

The Witch's Star

SUBMITTED BY BAILEY

For my whole life I've been very intrigued by paranormal things. When I was twelve years old, I had a few friends come over while my mom was not home. We made something that I like to call a witch's star. I'm not sure if that's the actual name for it, but I'll describe what it is. We would take dirt from the earth and make a big star out of it. Then from there, I took jarred candles and put one on every point of the star, and one free-standing candle on a plate in the middle. We put three shot glasses in the three top parts of the star filled with air, water, and the blood of a virgin.

We all sat in a circle holding hands and began to start asking questions. We weren't really getting any responses, so we started egging the spirits on, saying not-so-good things like, "Nobody's here, so you guys can't really do anything," or "Oh, you're not strong enough to do this or that." Everything then went downhill when the free-standing candle started to move!

At first, the flame on the candle grew to about two feet tall. Then it went down to the point where it was just about to go out, and then it went back up again. It did that a few times before the flame literally made a ninety-degree angle and started to spin around in a circle! Of course we all freaked out and, right as we were going to stand up and turn the lights on, my friend's phone that had been sitting on the table far away from us was thrown across the room!

Nothing else happened that night, but this would be the beginning of something that felt evil following me from twelve years old to now twenty-seven years old.

It wasn't until about a year later that little things started to happen. I would hear what I thought was my cat stuck in the attic—the frantic scratching of claws and movement at the bottom of the attic door, which was in my bedroom. Then, when I went to open the door, nothing would be there, and each time I found that my cat had actually been outside the whole time. I also heard something whisper my name into my ear when I was in the shower. Whatever it was, it did not sound human, and I could literally feel its breath. My friends and I also heard a noise in the hall like someone was walking by, just dragging their nails along the walls. Things would get moved and thrown, and people would get scratched while in my bedroom. But the scariest thing to happen was probably two years after these strange things first began, when I was fourteen.

My friends and I would sometimes smoke in my attic when my mom wasn't home. We had an old table and chairs set up so we could hang out up there. One day, I had them over as I often did, and we were alone because my mom was working nights at that time. We had just finished smoking, so we pushed all the chairs into the table and went downstairs. It was about 5:00 p.m. at this point. I was doing the dishes, just talking to my friend Ashton, when we both heard what sounded like someone walking in the attic. We went into the living room to ask our other two friends, Becca and Mary, if they were hearing it, too, but they said no. When it happened two more times, Ashton and I told them to come into the kitchen and listen. That's when all four of us heard what sounded like very heavy feet walking in the attic. It just kept getting louder and louder, and then it also sounded like the chairs were being dragged across the floor!

We all freaked out and went into the living room, and we were still able to hear it. Ashton tried to call her boyfriend to come over, but he wasn't picking up, so she called her boyfriend's best friend Dylan, and before he could even answer the phone, we heard this very loud and very inhuman scream come over the phone! She hung up and called him right back and asked him, "Dude, are you fucking with me? Why would you scream like that?" and he said, "What the hell are you talking about? As soon as I answered the phone, you hung up on me before I could even say hello."

At that point, Becca was so scared that she was crying and called her mom to come get her. Ashton, Mary, and I just tried our best to ignore the sounds. They finally slowed down around 8:00 p.m., but at 2:00 a.m. they started to pick back up, and at that point we were done. We had my gram come get us and we stayed the night at her house. I locked all the doors when I left, so no one was in the house from 2:00 a.m. until 10:00 the next morning. When I got home, I wanted to see if the chairs in the attic had actually been moved, so I slowly walked up the stairs to check. All eight chairs had been moved the whole way across my big attic, and some had even been knocked over!

Night in the Woods

SUBMITTED BY KRYSTA

In 2011, I moved back in with my parents after a bad breakup. While I was staying with them, I was living it up with new friends over the summer, trying to forget about my ex. My friend—we'll call her Mary—and I had heard of a nearby water hole on a lazy river that sounded like a good time, so we thought we would spend the day there, have a couple of drinks, and see if we could meet some cute boys. This place ended up being much farther away than I thought it was going to be, about forty-five minutes from my house, but we were already committed, so I drove out there and we wound our way through one of the many state parks in Missouri.

We really had no idea where we were going, but the moment we passed the river, we decided to park in the closest lot and walk a trail along the riverbank to see if we might run into people. Sure enough, after about a five-minute walk along the river, we saw a large group of people and asked if we could hang out with them. We joined them, and everyone was having fun in the sun, so we completely lost track of time. Before we knew it, someone mentioned that the sun was going to set soon and that we all needed to haul ass back to our cars. Everyone started walking to the parking lot through the shallow side of the river, but then some boy said something along the lines of "Watch out for water snakes," and I immediately noped out of the river. My friend Mary also hopped out, and we decided to just walk on the trail path that was directly next to the river, which was how we had initially gotten there.

Almost like someone turned off a light switch, the moment we hopped on the trail it got dark *fast*. And then we somehow managed to fall a little behind the group and could no longer see them. We could still hear their voices, though, so we followed along. After a few minutes of this, Mary and I noticed that we had been walking on the path for a really long time and thought that there was no way we'd walked that far when we walked in. It was at this point that we realized we could no longer hear anyone's voices and that the sunlight was almost completely gone. Fear began to creep in: we were wearing only our swimsuits and flip-flops, we had no idea where we were, and we were about to be stranded in the dark. We thought maybe we had gone too far and overshot the parking lot, so we backtracked along the trail, trying to see if we might stumble on my car. If you haven't been deep in a state park after dark, it's easy to lose your bearings, even if the path is easily navigable during the day. The trees completely closed in on us, blocking the light from the moon and stars—and of course there was no artificial light, nothing. It was so dark that I could not see my hand directly in front of my face. It was like being stuck in a vacuum. Not only that, but all the warmth from the day had completely evaporated, and we were absolutely freezing.

I know at this point you're probably thinking *Why don't you call someone to come help you?* but we had both left our cell phones in my car, knowing we'd be spending the day in the water. We sat there for a moment, unsure of what to do, and the thoughts of water snakes, animals, and every other possible scary thing began racing through our brains. We were desperate to find my car, and it was at this point that we decided to split up—Mary continued down the path away from the water hole, and I continued to backtrack. We figured that surely one of us would stumble upon the parking lot, and from there it would be easy to get back to the main road to find help, or go back into the woods and retrieve the other. We would periodically shout out to each other, so we would know where the other was.

I have no idea how it happened, but at some point as we were shouting to each other, I realized that not only was she almost completely out of earshot, but somehow the trail I was on was taking me up a very large hill. This did not seem right at all, as we'd never encountered a hill on our way in, and so I sort of panicked and decided to head back and follow her voice. The moment I turned around, I tripped over something and tumbled down the hill, tore up my arms and legs on prickly bushes, and twisted my ankle. In the process of falling, I lost my flip-flops, so now I was barefoot in the forest, alone, in nothing but a swimsuit, with a possibly sprained or maybe even broken ankle. I tried walking on my foot—I really did— but it hurt so bad, and at this point I was terrified of falling again and making my injury worse, so I sat down. I called out to Mary and told her I was injured and that I couldn't keep walking. After an hour or so of calling back and forth to each other in the dark, she found me, and we decided to stay put together on the trail until sunrise. In all that time apart, Mary had never come across a parking lot, let alone my car, and to continue searching would only have put us at risk of getting more hurt or more lost.

This is when things got weird. I told Mary that we could take shifts sleeping and that she could go first, but I knew deep down that there was no way in hell I'd be able to sleep out there. So I sat up alert, in pain, listening to the crickets and frogs in the forest, going back over everything in my mind and trying to figure out where we'd gone wrong. After about an hour of sitting there, I noticed something really off. There were no sounds at all—nothing: no frogs, no cicadas, no crickets, no movement, just complete silence. I said something about it to Mary, but realized that she had fallen asleep, so it was just me. I told you before how it was so dark I couldn't see my own hand in front of my face. Well, that hadn't changed. I couldn't distinguish the path we were on, I couldn't make out trees or bushes, all I saw was pitch-black. I felt this really ominous vibe like something evil was watching us, and the hair on the back of my neck stood up. All I could think was, *This is how people die mysteriously in the woods.*

Suddenly everything began to shift—from eerie and evil to almost protective, like someone or something was placing a shield around us. It was in this moment that I saw the first thing I was able to see since the sun had set hours ago: some figures emerged about a football field away and, although there was no moonlight, they were illuminated. They were almost pale silverish blue, and they were so skinny! At first I thought they were deer, but when I studied them more closely I realized that whatever they were, each figure was standing on two legs and had a head similar to you and me, but much skinnier than humans. I didn't feel any fear when I looked at them. In fact, all I felt was complete peace and safety, like they were watching over us. I thought my mind had to be playing tricks on me and that maybe I was just looking at trees—but they were moving! They moved like you and I might move if we were adjusting our weight from one hip to the other. It looked like maybe they were having a conversation with each other, probably wondering what to do with these two dumb humans who had stumbled into their forest. I stared at them and they stared back at me, just watching each other for about fifteen minutes or so. It was like they were as curious about us as we were about them, but they stayed at a distance. The next thing I knew, I could hear crickets and frogs again, and then shortly after that, the figures disappeared back into the darkness. From there, I fell in and out of consciousness until I finally opened my eyes to daylight.

I was able to get a good look at my ankle, and it was incredibly swollen and purple. If I tried to put any weight on it, I would fall over in pain. Mary had wandered down the path a little way to search for our car when she heard a man calling out to us—someone had sent out a search party when they saw that my car was still in the parking lot from the night before. From there, somehow they were able to get us both on a golf cart and drove us on a gravel path back to my car. Oddly enough, the path back to the car was a fifteen-minute drive, so I have no idea how far off we ended up—but we had backtracked way beyond the water hole. I still have no idea what I saw that night, but I know that whatever it was had been watching us and protecting us from something else. I have learned so much about general preparedness and safety since this event, and will never enter a park without proper gear again.

That's Not Her Teacher

SUBMITTED BY ANONYMOUS

Two years ago, my wife and I decided to enroll our three-year-old daughter in a Montessori school. We were introduced to the woman who would turn out to be her main teacher. Let's call her Ms. Jane. She was, in my opinion, just a few years older than me, so late thirties, max.

After a few months, Ms. Jane made an announcement, saying she was taking a leave of absence so she could take care of her mother. We said our goodbyes. My daughter really loved Ms. Jane and was so sad to see her go.

Six months went by. I did my usual morning drop-off, and the person at the door was so excited to see my daughter, saying, "Hey, remember me?! I missed you so much!" I glanced at my daughter, and I could tell she had *no* clue who this lady was. This lady realized my daughter needed a reminder and said, "It's me, Ms. Jane!" and gave her a big hug. I smiled it off and left. I got in my car and had to get my thoughts in order because *that* was *not* Ms. Jane. I was completely lost on my drive home, because this lady was much older—I'd say early sixties at least. She had a humpback and dressed like an older person. The Ms. Jane I knew did not have a hump on her back and dressed to impress with her hair done all the time.

At this point, I hadn't told my wife, because I knew she would think I was an idiot who didn't even remember what they'd had for breakfast. I had to make sure I wasn't losing it and make sure I'd heard her name correctly.

At the end of the day, the teachers usually tell me how the day went. That day, it was the same lady from the morning at the door. She greeted me and then told me how my daughter was so great and knew so much for her age, and I immediately said, "Oh, you should have seen her when she first started." A confused look crossed the woman's face, and she said, "Oh, I know. I was there, remember?" I replied, "Oh yeah, haha," but in my head I was thinking, *There's no way in hell you're that same person. NO WAY.*

Once we got home, I finally told my wife what had happened; as predicted, she wrote me off, saying, "Well, you know makeup makes a person look much younger than they are. You just forgot." I told her there's no way these two were the same person, but again she laughed it off.

Two weeks went by. One afternoon, my wife had to pick up our daughter since I couldn't that day. When she got home, she looked as though she had seen a ghost. She said to me, "There's no fucking way that's Ms. Jane! I'm in shock right now! Who the hell is that person?! She looks nothing like Ms. Jane. That was a random old lady." It was a good feeling to know that I wasn't batshit crazy. We moved not long after that and sent our daughter to a new school. No teacher glitches there. Things are normal.

Here's the wild part. Yesterday, my daughter, who's five now, told me how she misses her friends and teachers at her old school and began to list all their names, but no mention of Ms. Jane. I asked her, "Wow, I can't believe you remember everyone's names. What about Ms. Jane? Don't you miss her?" My daughter gave me a weird look, as if I were testing her memory. She replied, "Who's Ms. Jane?" She was very serious. I looked through their school website and through all her pictures so I could remind her, but I can't find a picture of Ms. Jane anywhere.

Revived

SUBMITTED BY ABBY

Every time I tell this to my family and friends, they think it was all just a dream, but I know I lived it. I just *know*.

I woke up on a Saturday morning with plans to hang out with my then-boyfriend, who was always awake earlier than me on weekends fixing cars and whatnot. For some reason, that morning I messaged him to let him know I was on my way even though I usually liked surprising him. I got ready and headed out his way. I vividly remember the time: it was 8:00 a.m., because my alarm was definitely set for that time. That's when I texted my boyfriend that I would go see him. So it must have been around 8:45 when I headed out of my house.

My boyfriend lived in a pretty sketchy area. When I got to his house, I pulled into his long driveway and noticed him talking to a man. I didn't think much of it, because he had friends over all the time. I parked my car but heard my boyfriend telling me to get back inside. The man he was talking to was actually not a friend, and they were not talking, they were arguing. The man was pointing a gun at him. I just did not see it when I drove up, as the man's back was facing the entrance of the driveway.

I tried to get back in the car to call the police, but the man shouted at me to go stand next to my boyfriend. My boyfriend kept yelling to get in the car. It all happened in a rush, but to this day I can still remember how *real* everything felt. It wasn't a dream. Everything was real life. I can't explain how I know it wasn't a dream, but I just know it wasn't. In an instant, I heard a gunshot and my brain informed me and prepared me for death. The man pointed his gun at me and I felt heat in my head. It felt like a huge hot balloon inside my head. I thought, *Okay, this is it, it's crazy, but this is how I'm dying.* I remember that I accepted my death quickly, and with what little consciousness I had I started praying, and even laughed at how cowardly I was to pray the last seconds of my life. Even though I'd always had my doubts about religion, that day I didn't. I fell to the dirt. I remember the heavy feeling of death. It felt like a big truck crushing my body. I was fading and prepared myself to find out what came after death. Moments passed, and I was still floating in nothingness, waiting for something to happen.

I woke up, insanely disoriented with a huge headache. It was Saturday at 10:00 a.m., and my alarm had been turned off at 8:00 a.m. I couldn't believe it was a dream. I *couldn't.* I checked my phone, and sure enough, my text message was there. It was all there. I called my boyfriend and asked him if he was okay. He said he was waiting for me to get there so we could go eat, and that he had the worst migraine in the world.

To this day, I really believe I died and God reset my clock and just decided it was not my time to go.

Keep Out

SUBMITTED BY ANGIE

One late afternoon when I was around seven, I was having a play-date with one of my friends. She had an idea to make signs to put on our bedroom doors that said, "Do not enter my room" (or something along those lines), as a way to playfully rebel against our parents. We spent a lot of time perfecting our signs, despite both our mothers laughing at our efforts. My mum in particular told me not to put it up, as it was "tacky." However, seven-year-old me thought I was really keeping up with the trends, so I decided to put it on my door after my mum went to bed later that night.

That night, I woke up only to witness a figure walking toward my open door. It was extremely dark in my hallway, but the figure contrasted with it starkly: it was white, with a large circular bobble-head and a stick-figure body. I was in utter shock, and I distinctly remember putting my hands around my eyes to ensure that I was both awake and seeing correctly. The figure continued to my door, then halted as it saw the sign. It stood there for a good five to ten seconds reading the words. I remember being extremely confused, thinking that it must've been my mother checking up on me, as she didn't approve of my sign. The figure then turned its body toward me, its head with no outlines for facial figures. It then looked back at the sign again, almost as if I blocked it from entering and therefore protected myself. It then *sprinted* out. I kid you not: it ran extremely fast down my hallway as I lay sitting upright in my bed facing my door, both stunned and confused.

In disbelief, I went back under my covers and slept straight through the rest of the night.

In the morning, I awoke and headed toward my mum, who was in the kitchen making breakfast. I asked her, "Why did you come to my room last night?" She was confused and remained quiet before saying that she hadn't gone to my room, or even woken up, at *all* during the night—which, for context, is extremely unlike her, as she is a light sleeper and often heads to the bathroom in the middle of the night. I told her that I saw someone come to my room during the night. She was shocked, and I told her what had happened. There was no one else in my house that night except me and my mum. My mother has had her own share of many paranormal experiences and is very open to the spiritual plane. She said that it was probably a ghost of some sort, and my sign perhaps stopped the entity from entering my bedroom as a precaution.

At the time, I wasn't too concerned; however, as I look back upon that day, I think that I was supposed to make that sign for a reason. The entity 100 percent wanted to come into my room, and I'm ever so grateful that I stopped any malicious events from occurring.

NO ONE WAS THERE

Stuck in a Loop

Submitted by Andriah

I live in a small(ish) town about thirty minutes north of Nashville, Tennessee. I work in Franklin, which is about fifty minutes away from home when there's no traffic; in rush-hour traffic it takes about an hour and twenty minutes to get home.

One day in March 2023, I was leaving work and I called my best friend McKenzie, like I do every day on my way home, and started talking to her. It was just our normal banter, talking about different aspects of life. There was more traffic than usual, and I was frustrated with the way people were driving, so I commented on it periodically. I had been on the road for almost an hour and was in standstill traffic. I looked up at the sign over the road and told Kenz that I was only just now at exit 85, and she told me, "Man, that sucks. I'm sorry." We continued talking and traffic started to thin out. She asked me if I was any closer, and I told her yes and that I was now passing exit 95 and traffic was better. For reference, from exit 95 I was only about twenty minutes from home.

She started to say what sounded like "Oh, that's good," but there was suddenly static on the line and I heard a weird deep voice under the static say, "No further," and then the line went dead. I tried calling her back but my phone kept displaying a *call failed* error message. I was focused on calling her back for a minute or two and was not paying attention to where I was, but at this point I should have been coming up on exit 98. I gave up on trying to call her back and started looking around and realized it was dark outside, even though it had been very bright two minutes earlier. Suddenly I saw a road sign that said ROSA L. PARKS BLVD., EXIT 85.

It was then that I realized I was the only vehicle on the road! There were no cars on either side of the interstate, no cars off the exit or on the bridges, and if you know Nashville, you know that this area is always busy no matter the time. I looked at my actual phone because I had been connected to my car and was just using the screen to call McKenzie previously, and my phone said *no service*. But the time on the phone was still 4:21 p.m. I was scared and was trying to legitimize it in my mind, thinking that perhaps a solar eclipse had caused the change in the light—maybe, I told myself, I had just missed the news about it. But something didn't seem right, and I was terrified. I tried calling my husband, but again it said *call failed*. I tried calling Kenz back, but my phone would not connect to any call. So I just decided to focus on getting home.

I was coming up on the 24/65 split. As soon as I went right on 65, I was back at exit 85! There were still no cars anywhere. I started speeding. I was going ninety-five miles an hour, because I knew I needed to make it home. I saw the split coming up again, and I sped up even more, thinking, *I just have to make it past this point*—but once again, as soon as I went right on 65, I was back at exit 85! So I changed my strategy. This time I decided I was going to go left onto 24. Surely that would get me somewhere different, right? So I sped up once again, and when I got to the split, I went left and started going around the curve. I thought for sure I was finally free, but as soon as I got around the curve, I saw ROSA L. PARKS BLVD., EXIT 85.

I started crying and I didn't know what to do, so I tried pulling over just because I was crying so hard at that point that I needed to breathe, *but I couldn't pull over!* My car physically would not stop! I pressed on the brakes a thousand times and they wouldn't work! So I tried to intentionally wreck my car. I know that sounds crazy, but I was just trying anything to pull me out of this. But my car was not reacting to my jerking the steering wheel or pressing the brakes at all—it was as though it was driving itself. I started screaming in panic, because I just didn't know what to do or if I was ever going to get out of this.

At this point I had to have been on the road for at least three hours, and I just kept going either way at the split to end up back at exit 85, with absolutely no one in sight, in a dark world where my phone was still stuck on 4:21 p.m. I was thinking about how I would never get to see my kids or my husband again. I started crying with my head in my hands while my car was driving itself on this endless loop—when, out of nowhere, static came over the speakers of my car and I heard "Continue" in that same deep voice behind the static. Instantly, as though someone had flipped a light switch, it was light out again, there were cars on the road, and I was passing *exit 98!* I looked down at my phone, and it said 4:22 p.m.! I knew I was out of that loop finally!

I called McKenzie back and she swore we had only been off the phone for thirty seconds, but she could hear in my voice that I had been crying and was very upset. I got home and basically kissed the ground as I got out of the car! I told my husband about what had happened, and he giggled and said I probably dozed off at the wheel for a minute and had a bad dream. I still can't figure out why or how it happened, but I know that it did. I'm still terrified every day on my way home from work that it's going to happen again.

Ouija Board Nightmare

SUBMITTED BY CORI

When I was probably around ten or eleven years old, I got invited to a sleepover at a girl in my class's house because she was having a big slumber party for her birthday. Let's call her Taylor. We weren't great friends, and I didn't know her that well, so I decided to ride with another friend of mine who I was closer to, let's call her Kendall, since she knew Taylor better than I did.

We were hanging out at her house, and at some point during the slumber party we decided to play with a Ouija board. I had never heard of a Ouija board and didn't really understand the concept. I just thought it allowed you to "talk to ghosts."

We started messing around with it; at first nothing happened, but eventually the planchette slowly felt like it started moving on its own. Eventually it got to the point where Taylor was the only one touching the planchette, and it was moving a lot faster. As time went on, and as we asked it more questions, it moved faster and faster. At one point, I noticed that Taylor's eyes weren't just looking down at the board, but they were *actually closed*. I thought that was a bit weird, considering you'd have to be looking to correctly move the planchette around the board to answer questions, especially if you were faking it.

All of us thought she was faking it and moving it herself, so my friend Kendall and I decided we were going to ask her something she didn't know. Since we didn't know Taylor very well, we knew she wouldn't know our friend Liz. So we asked her what Liz's phone number was. *She got it right. Even the area code.* We all got creeped out immediately, and we started to ask it more serious questions, considering that we were now convinced it was a real spirit. We found out the spirit's name was Spencer and he'd died when he was twenty-two from some sort of disease. We did this for a couple of hours, talking to our new friend while Taylor sat completely silent with her eyes shut, moving the planchette by herself almost as if this spirit was channeling through her in order to communicate with us. Spencer at some point started getting a little aggressive and angry, so we kept moving the planchette to GOODBYE, but Taylor would instantly reset it to HELLO.

We were getting creeped out and begged her to stop. The planchette started shuffling around the board too fast for us to read, and Taylor started to shake until she was having a full-blown seizure. We screamed for help and one of the girls, who was more familiar with Taylor's parents and house, ran to get Taylor's parents, but their bedroom door was locked. She banged on the door until they came out, rushed into Taylor's room, and called an ambulance.

They had us all sit in the living room while they shut the door and worked on bringing Taylor back to consciousness.

After the paramedics arrived and everything started calming down, the girl who had run to get Taylor's parents asked them, "Why did you guys lock your door?! You never usually shut it! I couldn't get you guys to wake up!" They both stopped in their tracks and looked at her and replied, *"We didn't shut the door."*

I don't play with them anymore.

Falling Rain

SUBMITTED BY SASKIA

When I was around seven years old, my family and I used to holiday at a caravan (camper) park in the summer (English people love a caravan, lol). The site was for caravan owners and some general holidaymakers. You couldn't get onto the site without going through security gates and being checked, so everyone knew everyone, and it was an all-around very safe place to be and play.

My cousin and I, along with our friend group, were exploring the site one day and came across an old, abandoned building. We'd never seen it before, but it was behind hedgerows and a huge tree that, if you climbed it, you could see the caravans closest to it. The building was all locked and boarded up. You couldn't go inside, and we all had a feeling that we shouldn't be there. Being mischievous, we translated that feeling into a sign that this was going to be our gang's new secret hideout. For some reason, we called it "The Bomb Shelter," and we never told our mums or the rest of the family about it.

This was all going swimmingly for a few weeks. Then one day our little gang went to "The Bomb Shelter" and I got an awful feeling that something was really, really wrong. And this time it was eerily wrong. I looked at the rest of the group, and it was clear that they all felt it, too. I was about to suggest going back to the playground in the main central area of the site, when we heard knocking. We looked around, thinking it must've been one of us playing a trick on the others, but it happened again, this time louder and more aggressive. *It was coming from inside the building!* We all froze in disbelief, and, as the thumping continued, a man's voice started shouting, *"Get away or I'll get you! Go go go!"* Screaming at us! Terrified, we all shrieked and got on our bikes, but as we went to ride off, *all* of the chains came off our bikes. Some of the chains even snapped!

As we were frantically trying to put the chains back on and get the hell out of there and away from the screaming man, the heavens opened, and it rained bucketloads—the type of rain where it bounces off the floor and hurts when it hits your bare skin and you can't see your hand in front of your face. Now I know I'm talking about July in England, but this was a downpour like I've never seen before or since, and we were completely drenched! We managed to get some of the chains back on our bikes, but those who couldn't just *ran* with us back to my caravan about a two-minute bike ride away. It actually only took us about thirty seconds this time, because of the adrenaline.

We all piled in, and we were all trying to tell my mum what had happened. She stopped us and asked, "Where have you been, and why are you absolutely drenched?!" We were confused, saying that we had been caught in the thunder and the rain. She said, "There was no rain or thunder. It's been brilliant sunshine all day." We had no choice but to take her back to the place and show her ourselves. The ground was completely dry the whole walk back, and when we got to where the building had been, *it was nowhere to be found!*

To this day, I cannot explain what happened, why the rain only fell on us, why all the bike chains came off and then broke at the same time, or where the building went.

We are all in our twenties now. I called my cousin before writing this to make sure that it hadn't gotten embellished in my little girl brain. But all I had to say was, "Do you remember The Bomb Shelter down the caravan?" and he recounted everything back to me exactly as I remembered it. He also cannot explain what happened.

Voice in My Head

SUBMITTED BY SANJA

Weird things have happened to me since childhood. For example, sometimes I hear a male voice inside my head that I can just talk with, or shut down completely if I want to. I have always considered that normal since it was always present, even though my mom told me not to tell anyone. She took me to the doctor when I was six, but the doctor didn't find any reason for it and told my mom that I probably just had an imaginary friend. I learned fast that people do not consider this normal and that I should not tell anyone about it.

My thought in older years was that I was probably schizophrenic; but, as I already said, I could just shake that voice out of my head, so when I didn't want to hear it I just pushed it down. Years went by and I totally forgot about it, until one day.

I was sixteen and was having a night out with my cousin, her brother, and his friends. My cousin and I had a lot of drinks (drinking age in my country is sixteen) before deciding we'd had enough. Since her brother was with some girl and didn't want to leave yet, he asked his two friends to take us home. The moment I sat in the back seat, I heard loud and clear in my head, almost like yelling, "Put the seat belt on!"

My cousin almost laughed at me because I was in the back seat and at that time it was not really normal to put a seat belt on when you sat there. The '90s were really not great years for safety in my country. But I left it on, in spite of her skepticism.

As it turned out, this was a good decision. It was the middle of the winter, and our car slipped on the ice and hit a concrete wall. Everyone survived, but I was the only one without any injuries. I was in shock, so I didn't think much of it until later on.

Fast-forward to a few years later, when I was twenty. I was already married (yeah, I know, I got married early), and one cold day I fell asleep in the living room. My husband was going to work and felt bad for me sleeping in the cold room, so he turned up the heat before he left. While sleeping, I heard loud and clear a male voice calling my name twice, a sound like someone smashing a hand on a table, and then, *"Wake up!"*

I turned around, expecting to see my husband, but no one was there. I sat up, and then it hit me—the smell of gas filled the room. There was a leak somewhere. I couldn't stand up. I crawled to the balcony door on all fours, opened it, put my head through, and passed out. My husband came back home because he couldn't find his phone, and he found me like that. Strangely, he said he had looked all over the car and his bag for the phone, and after everything, he found it sitting on the front seat of his car, out in the open.

There were more situations where I felt someone watching over me, like just before I got fired. I was sitting alone and felt a physical hand on my shoulder, like it was trying to comfort me before something bad happened. But the most vivid thing was the moment I was giving birth.

My brother had died a couple of months before I was due to deliver my first child, and my depression was horrible. In that moment, I really didn't want to live anymore. There were complications during the birth, and they sent me for an emergency cesarean. I have no idea what the anesthesiologist did wrong, but I woke up in the middle of it. I was lucky that I'd gotten an epidural when they were trying to have me give birth naturally, because otherwise it would have been incredibly painful. I tried to signal to them somehow that I was awake, but I couldn't. Then I heard a beeping sound from the monitor above me—I suppose I fell into cardiac arrest, and it felt like someone pushed me from the back. There was no tunnel of light or life passing in front of my eyes. I was just there one minute, and then the next I was somewhere else.

I didn't remember anything. I just knew that I was *there* now, and that I'd had a life before that. The place where I found myself hypnotized me: endless darkness with a huge light in the middle and small ones moving around it; something like how we present atoms in pictures. I was me, but I wasn't. It felt like I was home. I felt peace and love that can only be described as complete nirvana.

And then the big light focused its attention on me. I don't even know how to explain it. In my essence, the question appeared: "Do you want to live?" I felt that I had to choose. I found myself thinking that life was bad and that I had never felt peace like this, and that I wanted to stay. But before I even finished thinking about it, my physical body connected to me somehow, and I felt my eardrums shaking like when you listen to music on the highest volume. That same voice that I'd heard so many times in my life said, *"Do you want to know your child?!"*

It was so strong that it reached me, and all of a sudden my mind was flooded with memories of the pregnancy. I will be honest, I didn't want to live—I wanted to stay there where I was—but the thought of leaving a baby behind without a mother shook me.

I didn't even manage to produce the thought (about wanting to go back) before the big light, as if it knew what I was thinking, just sent me there. I felt that I was in my body now, and that it was not breathing. I collected the last atom of energy I possessed to start it again. We live with pain every moment of our life, and we are so used to it that we ignore it. But forcing every muscle in my body to flex and take that first breath was painful as hell.

Then I didn't feel anything anymore. I was asleep. The next thing I remember is waking up with the nurse putting a pillow behind my head. She told me that I'd given them the scare of their lives and that she was glad to see me awake.

I changed a lot after that experience. I am not afraid of dying—in fact, I feel more alive than ever. I haven't heard the voice since that experience, maybe because nothing bad has happened, or maybe I just became stronger and no longer need its guidance. But it is comforting to have the knowledge that someone somewhere is keeping me safe.

Alien Text Message

SUBMITTED BY TREA

One summer day back in 2016, my older sister and I were sitting outside. She got a phone call from her best friend, who was clearly upset, saying something insane had happened with her father.

Her father said he was watching TV and it was about an hour or so after the sun had gone down. His two dogs were outside in the front yard, and they started going crazy as if they were trying to tell him that someone was outside. Not a big deal really, because they tend to do that whenever anyone passes by. But as he started to go check it out, he said that the TV seemed to have lost the signal and it was just static. That was the last thing he was absolutely sure about, and then he "came to" and the sun was again setting in the sky. He was confused by that, because he was sure that he had just watched the sun set before sitting down to watch his show.

He checked his cell phone, and he had several missed calls from many people. Even his boss had texted him and asked if he would be coming in to work that day. His daughter said that she had gone over to his house earlier in the day, and he was nowhere to be found. His car was there, and the keys were on the counter. She even said that the shoes he would wear around the house were on the floor at the foot of his chair as if he was sitting there, but he himself was nowhere to be found.

Around the time he was waking up in the chair, a text message was sent from his cell phone to his daughter. It was a strange message, almost like a multimedia message; but when he talked to her about it later, she swore that some of the symbols in it were not even available on her phone. They called the phone company later to see if he'd really sent the message, and they said that they had no record of any messages sent out from his phone at that time. My sister had an idea, and said, "Forward it to me so that I can see the message." They hung up, and my sister got it a few seconds later. I know that it sounds crazy, but I literally watched from right beside her as she opened the message. As soon as she opened it, her phone shut off just like it had died, and that phone was done. It never worked again.

Eventually we did meet up with my sister's friend, and she showed us the message. It almost reminded me of Morse code, but somehow different. I asked her father what he could remember about the whole thing. He said that it was weird, because he was never one to remember his dreams, but when he was checking out the dogs, he was blinded by an overpowering light—brighter than anything he had ever seen. The only thing he could recall afterward was lying on a table like he was in surgery, and that the table was so cold that it made it hard to breathe. On both sides of him and standing at his head, there were what he thought were the doctors working on him. They had on full surgical suits and masks over their faces, so their eyes were the only thing that he could actually see for sure. He said that he must've been having a weird dream, because they had the eyes of a snake. And he said that when they were cutting him, there was a lot of blood, and if it had been real, he shouldn't have been alive.

I've always felt weird about what he told me, but I do know that he wouldn't make up something like this. He was always a nonbeliever about those sorts of things, and he would never say that he had seen aliens. I also know that my sister's phone was fine and worked great until the second she opened up that message. I'm still shook up about it, and I don't know what to think.

Haunted Mirror

SUBMITTED BY MEL

I am somebody who weird things have always happened to, so I have plenty of stories to share. On one particular day, I had just moved into my new apartment, and I was happily showing it to my sister. My bedroom came with a long mirror nailed to the back of the door. Other than that, the house was empty except for my boxes. After I gave her the tour, my sister and I were chatting in the kitchen when suddenly we heard a loud crashing sound coming from my bedroom. We both ran toward the sound and saw that the mirror on the back of the door had been completely shattered. I'm talking like cobwebbed splinters of glass, like someone took a hammer to it. There was nothing that could have broken the mirror, as we were the only two in the house: the room was empty, windows were all closed. I had no pets. There was no explanation for it. I even gently ran a finger over the large cracks in it, bewildered. Tiny shards of glass littered the rug around the bottom.

We shrugged, not knowing what had happened, and returned to the kitchen. As we were chatting again, for the second time we heard a loud crashing sound coming from my room. Just like before, we ran toward my room, and this time the mirror was completely intact. No cracks in the glass, no broken pieces. It looked brand-new. We both were standing there open-mouthed, staring at the mirror in shock. I let out a scream, and my sister said "Fuck this" and ran out of the room. We rummaged through some boxes until we found a screwdriver, and my sister took the mirror from behind my door and ran with it outside to toss it on the curb.

The next day was trash pickup and the mirror was gone. I don't know what any of this means, but I've never liked mirrors, and this is a good example as to why. After that, I always felt like I was being watched in that house.

Ghost Woman

SUBMITTED BY JOEI

In 2009, my mom moved us into an apartment next door to a cemetery. I have two other siblings who were four years old and nine months old at the time, and I was two years old. My aunt, who had many ghost experiences in her lifetime, was fifteen. She and my mom noticed little things when we moved in, like my younger brother screaming once they walked him into the bedroom. But it wasn't just that.

My aunt would often spend the night to watch us while my mom went to work. My aunt slept on the couch in the living room with a mirror facing the couch. She would feel something looking at her while she slept; one night when she opened her eyes, something ducked behind the couch, and she could hear the sound of someone running away.

On a different day, my aunt was watching us while my mom was away. We were at a park nearby, and she walked us back to the apartment to get drinks. When we got there, nobody else was at home. As we were about to walk out the door to go back to the park, something knocked on the bedroom door. My four-year-old brother went to reach for the doorknob, and my aunt yelled, "No, don't open it!" Then, turning to the door, she screamed, "I'm not scared of you—leave us alone!" Next thing you know, the bedroom door started banging and shaking as if the door was going to break down. My aunt ran us out of the apartment as fast as she could.

An hour later, we came back to the apartment. My mom was upset with my aunt because, she said, all the doors were open, including the front door, and all the lights were turned on. My aunt reassured my mom that when we left, only the kitchen light was on and all the doors were closed.

One night, my mom and aunt were having a conversation in the kitchen, and my aunt told my mom, "I'm going to use the restroom. I'll be right back." She went into the bathroom—and my mom was in there with me, doing my hair and getting me ready for bed. My aunt looked back into the kitchen, and nobody was there. When thinking back to her conversation with my "mom," she said that one thing she noticed was how my mom wouldn't look her in the eye the entire conversation.

On another day, my aunt and my grandfather walked my brother home. They lived down the street from us. My mom and I were on our way home but hadn't gotten there yet. They knocked on the door and heard my mom saying, "One second, be right there." They stood there for a couple of minutes and were confused because it was pitch-black inside and nobody had come to the door yet. They started to walk off, and then my grandfather remembered that they had a house key. He opened the door and, to their surprise, nobody was home. My grandfather started to walk toward the bedroom, but he stopped in his tracks and started walking back toward us slowly when he saw a woman in a long white dingy dress. Her eyes were black and her skin was pale, with the appearance of dirt smeared all over her body. She started walking toward my grandfather, and they ran out of the house. They ran into us in the parking lot, and we all started walking home together. As they were walking next to the cemetery, my aunt turned around to see the woman standing in the street.

My mom moved us out of there, but the woman had already attached herself to us. She was and is constantly seen by our family to this day, but she is mainly around my grandfather. He took a picture of the kitchen once, and you could see her crawling under the kitchen table.

Paranormal Childhood

SUBMITTED BY CAYTEE

The paranormal has always been in my life. My dad was a paranormal investigator and ran a very popular paranormal website in the '90s, so maybe that's why spirits have always been attached to my family.

The house my family grew up in was a typical Long Island home. An average-size four-bedroom home with a finished basement. The stairs going to the basement ended in the middle of the room, with the living-room area to the right. On the left, you could walk back farther in the basement, where we had a computer area, a bar, and a large cement laundry room in the very back.

This house had a lot of paranormal activity. If you were home alone and went into the basement, it sounded as if there was a casual get-together upstairs, with people walking back and forth, low murmuring, and even some glasses clinking here and there. Of course, if you rushed upstairs, nobody would be there. *Everyone* (my dad, mom, older sister, older brother, and myself) in the family experienced this.

One day I remember sitting in the computer area, playing a game on the computer, when I felt someone walk past me. I heard the loud plastic accordion door to the laundry room open and close, making its signature very distinct clicking noise. Then I heard the washing machine turn on. I didn't think anything of it. I figured my mom was doing laundry, so I began to talk to her and asked her a question. She didn't answer me, so I asked her again. She didn't answer. I got up, walked over to the laundry room, and opened the door. The room was dark, no one was in there, and the washing machine was not on. This exact same thing happened to my father a few weeks later.

Whenever we left the house for the day, there would always be something moved around when we got back. I remember one day during the Thanksgiving season when we came home to the decorative paper pilgrims my mother had placed on the windows turned around and upside down. This was particularly confusing because when we originally put them up, we taped all of their sides in place, and there wasn't any indication that the tape had been moved. My mother was sure that we were messing with her and one of us had done it. We hadn't.

One day we came home to a picture of me ripped up very carefully and put back together in a puzzle-like state on my mother's bed. She was so angry and demanded to know who had done this to the picture. No one had done it; no one had been in the house while we were out.

Then there was also the usual "haunted house" stuff—unplugged radios and cassette players turning on, TVs turning on and off randomly, sounds in closets, as well as lights going on and off.

The scariest thing I ever experienced in that house was when I was in my parents' room. They had a dresser that had a large mirror on top. I remember playing with my mother's jewelry on the dresser and looking up to suddenly see an old woman wearing white standing next to me, looking at me through the mirror. I was still very young, so this of course scared me to death. I ran and told my mother, and she comforted me and brushed it off.

I learned later in life that the house next to us had been the scene of a tragedy. An old woman and her son had lived next door, and one day the son had gone crazy and murdered her and set the house on fire. She died trying to crawl her way to the door; she never made it. I always thought this old woman had attached herself to our house, since hers burned down.

When I was a teenager, my family ended up building and then moving into a very large house directly across the street from the house we grew up in. We moved in and thought the paranormal activity would end. We saw it as a fresh start. We were wrong. The woman followed us.

This house was a very large two-story home. It had a basement as well, but not finished. It was the entire length of the house—just a huge, dark, cold cement basement with a two-car garage attached to it. You never wanted to go into that basement alone, especially at night. There was always this heavy feeling, and you would often hear and feel things. We still experienced lights going on and off and random electrical occurrences (TVs and radios turning on and off, and so on).

One night the whole family went out to dinner, and when we came home we could not find our small silky terrier. We called her name and looked everywhere, but she was nowhere to be found. My mother had a large master bedroom, with a massive walk-in closet that had built-in shelves up to the ceiling. I walked into the closet and called for the dog. I heard a little whimper and a candle fell off the top shelf. I looked up and the dog was sitting on the very top shelf, shivering. There is no way this tiny dog would have been able to get up there by itself.

By the time I was sixteen, my sister and brother had gone off to college and it was just me and my mom in the home. One day my mother left for work and I was getting ready to go out to the bus stop. I walked outside and looked back at the house, only to see the old lady standing in the window of my mother's room at the very top of the house. She was looking down, directly at me. I hurried to the bus stop and tried to forget about it. When I got home from school I carefully walked into my mother's bedroom, but never saw her in there again.

The absolute scariest experience happened in my mother's master bathroom. This was a very large bathroom. When you walked in, to the right was a very long counter with two sinks that led to the bathtub. On the left there was a half wall, the toilet, and the large shower recessed back into the wall. One day I had gotten home from school and was home alone. I decided to take a shower. I remember being in the middle of my shower and hearing the bathroom door open (the bathroom door had a very distinct creak). I turned around and *saw* the bathroom door open. Something wearing white walked in, walked very slowly past the shower, past the wall, toward the bathtub, turned around back toward the door, but stopped right in the middle of the bathroom, turned around, and faced me in the shower. The shower door was frosted, so I could only make out a wiggly white figure, looking in my direction. I froze, didn't move a muscle, and just stared back. It felt like forever, but eventually the white figure walked out and closed the door. I stayed in that shower for another hour because I was so scared.

After I graduated from high school I ended up getting pregnant, and my boyfriend (now husband) moved in with me and my mom in her house. My husband would always get a really bad feeling in this home. He would see spirits all the time and shadows of people who were not there. One night when it was snowing heavily, my husband woke up in a panic and said, "He's outside!" I tried to comfort him and sleepily told him, "There's no one here," as he often had night terrors. He jumped out of bed and looked out my bedroom window to the street and said he saw a tall black figure standing there in the middle of the street. He was terrified. I think I just told him to go back to bed as I thought he was just having a night terror, and I was very pregnant and very tired.

A year after my son was born, my mother had to sell that large house and move into a smaller, much older home. We moved with her, as we were a very young couple with a baby. This house was bad news. It was a small two-story house with a finished basement. The upstairs was a loft area with a large open living room, a small bathroom, a closet and two bedrooms. The basement had two cedar closets, a laundry room, a large living-room area and a bedroom that had a small closet with a very small bathroom attached. This laundry room had a small window to the bedroom bathroom. No idea why, but I hated it. So creepy!

We ended up moving into the basement. We put our infant son in the bedroom, and we slept in the living-room area on a pull-out couch every night. We would often have to rock our son to sleep in his rocking chair with the lights off and just the bathroom light on for the smallest amount of light. The rocking chair was set up right in front of the closet. It was a wooden bifold closet and didn't fully close for some reason. There were nights when our son would just scream and scream, which was usually not like him. We stopped rocking him and would attempt to look him in the face, but he would always be looking *past* us with his eyes *locked* onto the pitch-black, slightly open closet, looking horrified. We would try to move his gaze from it, but he would just stare, wide-eyed, crying. We would take him out to the living room and let him fall asleep with us on nights like that.

One night, I was rocking him to sleep. He was pretty calm and dozing off when all of a sudden a figure walked past the light in the bathroom. I brushed it off, as I was just tired and thought I was imagining things, but moments later it happened again: a figure slowly walking past the bathroom light. I quietly brought my son out into the living room and told my husband what had just happened. He stopped and looked at me like he had seen a ghost (pun intended). I said, "What?" He answered, "I didn't want to tell you, because I didn't want you to be scared, but I have been seeing that the last two nights. It's the same black figure I saw in the snow at the other house." We moved to the upstairs loft area shortly after that.

There was such a bad, heavy feeling in that basement. Moving upstairs was a better feeling—not much happened upstairs, but the house was still very haunted. At this point I would be home alone a lot with my son, as my husband and mother had to work. There were many times where I heard my mom or husband come home (door opening, keys jingling, footsteps) and I would call down from the loft, only to discover that no one had come home at all and I was still alone. Often, when my son went down for a nap, I would do laundry, which meant going to the basement. Remember that weird window from the laundry room to the bedroom bathroom? While I was loading the washer, my back was to the dark window (the bathroom was no longer being used, as the bedroom was now full of random storage). I heard two loud knocks on the window! I spun around and could only see darkness. I turned the washing machine on and ran upstairs as fast as I could. I called my husband and asked him where he was, as I was sure he was playing a prank on me. He told me he was still at work. I didn't go back down to switch the laundry that night. This happened a few more times during the time we lived there.

I could go on and on about this house. *So* many weird occurrences and always such a heavy, bad feeling. We ended up moving out after my second son was born. I will note that a few years ago, my mother's basement ended up flooding and they had to redo the entire thing. Once the renovation was done, that heavy feeling was gone. The dresser that used to be in both of my mother's master bedrooms (where I saw the old woman in the mirror and then in the window) was destroyed in the flood. I would bet that the old woman attached herself to it, and now that it's gone, she's gone.

Another weird side note: in the basement bedroom there was a large, long mirror that was the entire length of the back wall and went to the ceiling and halfway down the wall. When they renovated the basement, they took down the mirror, and behind it was a very large, dirt-filled terrarium, built into the wall. It was so big, you could easily crawl into and sit up in it if you wanted to. It was so freaky. I don't know what it was for, but I swear something very strange used to live in there.

My husband and I ended up moving several times to several states with our now-four children. We have experienced a few paranormal things here and there since then, but now I sage my house regularly to keep these things at bay.

Demon in My Dorm

SUBMITTED BY KAITLYN

I attended college at a very, very old private school in North Carolina. And by "old," I mean it was founded in the 1890s. So, as you can imagine, there's a lot of history there, and apparently some of that history is not so good. My roommate and I stayed in one of the oldest dorm buildings on campus our freshman year. And let me tell ya, that place was *haunted.* I have always believed in "the other side," but boy, did living in that place make me a true believer. The paranormal activity randomly started one day, and it just progressively got more intense.

I remember when it started. My roommate—we'll call her Mary—and I were just sitting on our beds doing homework like we always did in the afternoons. Our room was very small and only contained our two beds and two desks. Mary never used her desk to study, but rather to store items and place things on. In the middle of our studying, her deodorant and a package of chewing gum slid all the way off her desk onto the floor. These items had been sitting in the dead center of her desk, so we knew it wasn't just a "draft." It appeared as if someone had taken their hand and just slowly pushed these two things off the desk at the same time. Mary and I both saw this and just looked at each other with wide eyes. I asked Mary, "Ummm . . . did you see that!?" Mary replied, "Ummm . . . yeah." We both agreed not to pay much attention to it because we didn't want any unseen forces to see that we were frightened.

Little things like this happened almost daily in our dorm room. We just carried on like usual in hopes that it would eventually stop. At that time, we did not feel threatened or on edge being in there; not yet.

Christmastime came around, and we decided to decorate our room. We put up a very small tabletop Christmas tree on Mary's desk. We decorated it with cute mini round ornaments one day. We then left the room to go hang out with a friend down the hall. When we returned to our room a couple of hours later, the ornaments were scattered *all over* the room. It looked like someone had thrown them. They weren't just sitting under the tree or on the desk like they had uneventfully fallen off. They were *everywhere*. Across the room, even on our beds. No one had keys to our room except us. And why would anyone do this? It really freaked us out. So, in an attempt to protect ourselves, we decorated the room with signs that had Bible verses on them. We went to Hobby Lobby and purchased a cute decorative cross to hang up on our wall. We hung up that cross in the room, and it fell down numerous times. Thinking it was just due to faulty Command Strips, we decided to prop it up on the windowsill. The cross continued to fall over, but each time it was more forceful, appearing as if it was being knocked over by something. This is when we started getting really nervous that something in our dorm room wasn't so nice.

So, of course, what did our smart college-student butts do? We decided to try to communicate with this entity using a Ouija board. So smart, right?! We invited a couple of our friends to come to our room to have a session and try to talk to this thing. We asked a few questions and didn't get much out of it at first. Then one of our friends decided to start asking it things in a more provoking manner. She asked it to show itself, to which it replied, "If I show myself, you will be scared." She then asked it what it looked like, and it told us that it had all black eyes, long ragged black hair, and white skin. We asked its name, to which it replied, "Camama." Not creepy, right?! Our friend then stupidly said, "Well, if you're so scary and real, why don't you knock over that cross?" And I shit you not, that cross went flying across that room with such force that we all jumped up and ran out of that building as quickly as we could! We were scared out of our minds, and I wanted so badly to pack my crap and move out.

Mary and I had a friend who lived across campus. We'll call him Leroy. I told Leroy about all this haunting stuff, and he asked if he could borrow the Ouija board for a few days. Of course we weren't planning on using it anymore, so I gave it to him and told him to have fun. This is important: I didn't give him *any* specific information regarding what our "demon" had said during our session. After a few days, I asked Leroy if he had used the board. He said, "Yes, and it was spooky. It said its name is Camama." After this conversation, Leroy told me he was having dreams of Mary and me becoming possessed. This made Mary and me true believers that this thing was as real as you and I.

Our university was of the Lutheran faith and had an on-campus chapel and pastor. I reached out to our pastor in an email and told him about all the haunting things we had experienced, and asked if he would pray for us and come do a blessing of our room. He asked what dorm building we were in. When I told him, he replied, "Yep, I figured. I have heard of this happening before in that building." How insane is that?! Was it the Ouija board that had an entity connected to it? Or did this dorm have more bad history than good?

Cafeteria Time Jump

SUBMITTED BY LOUISE

I'm in the UK, and this happened back in secondary school. It was a normal school day, and it was warm and sunny outside. The bell for lunch rang, and I made my way to the cafeteria, got my lunch, sat at a table, and began to eat. I always sat by myself because I didn't have any friends and was very socially awkward.

I was partway through my lunch, which was just some chips and a slice of pizza, when I noticed it had started to rain. The cafeteria is in a separate building all on its own, and every side of the cafeteria has windows. I looked out the windows to my right and it was pouring down hard and fast. I looked out the windows to my left and it was bright and sunny. I looked around to see if anyone else was seeing this, but everyone was just chatting and going on as usual. Not a single person seemed to notice what was going on, so I tried to brush it off and resume eating.

The second I turned back to my plate, there was a loud crash of thunder. It was so loud, the whole building felt like it was shaking. On instinct, I closed my eyes and covered my ears. When I opened them again, it was pitch-black outside. I looked around, and I was completely alone in the cafeteria. I wondered if I had kept my eyes closed for longer than I thought and had missed the end-of-lunch bell. I picked up my plate, which was still warm; the food was still hot. I took it over to the serving counter. No staff around and no signs of lunch. I set my tray down and went to head out of the cafeteria, but the main door was locked. I was freaking out at this point, but I made my way to the fire exit, knowing that for a long while the alarm had been broken in that particular building.

I left and began to head to the building where my next class would be. The school grounds were bare and eerily quiet. As I passed the other buildings, I noticed they were all dark and empty. At this point, I changed my mind about going to where my next class would be, and decided to leave the school. The front gate was closed, so I had to find a way to climb over the fence and get out. Luckily this was the '90s and security was really bad, so it didn't take much to get out. I walked home, and the streets were empty and quiet. The shops were all closed. I was very scared at this point and shaking a little. I lived in a relatively small town, but still large enough that you would normally see a person or two walking around, even in the middle of the night.

I made it home, about a thirty- to forty-five-minute walk, and the door was locked. It was never kept locked, so I rang the bell, and after a few minutes my mother answered and started yelling at me, asking me where the hell had I been and why I was outside. I was confused and explained what had happened. She looked shocked, then told me I hadn't come home from school and they had contacted the police, who insisted that I was likely at a friend's and to contact them the next day if I hadn't shown up. Again, this was the '90s, a much more relaxed time. This is when I looked at the time and I saw that it was 3:00 a.m. My mother said we would talk more in the morning and to get to bed. So off to bed we went. The next day, my mother and father both asked me a lot of questions. I told them what had happened again, but they didn't believe me. I started to wonder if maybe I had fallen asleep in the cafeteria and I'm just so unnoticeable that no one saw me. However, I still couldn't explain how my food was still hot.

That day, I went to school as normal. At some point during the day, a girl I had never spoken to before came up and asked me what the hell had happened. I asked what she meant, and she explained that yesterday during lunch the canteen lights had suddenly flickered and she had happened to look in my direction. She saw me cover my ears, and then I was gone. She herself freaked out and wondered if she had seen a ghost, so she was scared when she saw me again today. We became friends after that, and I never had to eat lunch alone again. We are still friends to this day.

A Final Note from Auntie Matrix

That concludes this collection of crazy and creepy stories. Maybe as you were reading, you remembered something that made you question what was real and what was not. Maybe you remembered something scary, strange, or unusual that happened to *you*. If so, and if you would like the chance to share your experience with our community, you can email me at auntiematrix@gmail.com.

If you want more of this content, I have plenty! Make sure you are following me on my socials for new videos about all of your freakiest stories.

Acknowledgments

First and foremost, an obvious but highly necessary thank-you to every person whose story is featured on these pages. Without you, this book would quite literally not exist.

To each one of you who has ever submitted or will ever submit your story, thank you for having the courage and taking the time to share a part of your life that may not be accepted by most. I feel honored to have your permission to share them with the world. And to every member of our little community who listens, comments, supports, and validates with an open mind and an open heart, thank you for making them feel accepted. This group of beautiful humans makes me proud, and I am thankful for each and every one of you. I love you, glitches!

To Jess C., KDJO, Jen, Tawnya, Katie, Kim, Jess S., and all my other Live moderators, thank you for taking time out of your personal lives to make sure the chat is flowing and free of Tonys. And to Justin, for keeping us entertained with your cryptic jokes.

To @happycowprocessedcheese for nonchalantly calling me Auntie Matrix in the comment section one day; a nickname that has undoubtedly stuck.

To Nichole, author of "What Was in that Closet?", the first story to freak me out so much that I couldn't even finish reading it until daylight.

To psychic healer Jusstine K for appeasing my woo-woo side and letting me know the universe was in favor of my doing a book.

ACKNOWLEDGMENTS

To Kate Zimmermann for offering me the opportunity to put this book together and staying on top of me in the friendliest way possible. I'm not sure it would have ever gotten finished without you. And to Amanda Englander for pointing Kate in my direction.

To my five cats for keeping me company while I worked. And in this case, "keeping me company" shall be defined as 10 percent zoomies and 90 percent sleeping.

To my father, from whom I get my love of nature, and my mother, from whom I get my strength, thank you both for loving and supporting me through all the things.

To my sister and her wife, for being beautiful people, and also for being my two biggest hype men.

To my kids for keeping me young and silly and for making my heart full.

And last, but certainly not least, to my partner Phill for happily and lovingly accepting me in all my ever-changing forms and for being there always. You get me and, man, do I appreciate that more than you know. I love you the most.

About the Author

Jessica Castro, born and raised on Long Island, was nicknamed Auntie Matrix by her fans on social media. She is intrigued by all things spiritual and strange, and to date has received thousands of personal accounts from others detailing their weird unexplainable experiences. She shares these stories with the world in the hopes of opening the minds of others, and giving comfort, confidence, and validation to those who have experienced similar things. When not absorbed in reading the latest submissions, Jess loves camping, hiking, anything woo-woo, snuggling her horde of cats, binging shows with her partner, and having fun with her kids.

You can watch her on TikTok, Instagram, Facebook, and YouTube, or listen to her on all major platforms, including Apple Music and Spotify, by searching "tessicavision."

You can submit your own personal story by emailing her at auntiematrix@gmail.com.

You can join her glitch community on Discord by going to dsc.gg/auntiematrix.